Animal Farm Prophecy Fulfilled in Africa

A Call to a Values and Systems Revolution

Chiku Malunga

University Press of America,® Inc.
Lanham · Boulder · New York · Toronto · Plymouth, UK

4501 Forbes Boulevard
Suite 200
Lanham, Maryland 20706
UPA Acquisitions Department (301) 459-3366

10 Thornbury Road
Plymouth PL6 7PP
United Kingdom

British Library Cataloging in Publication Information Available

Library of Congress Control Number: 2014943365
ISBN: 978-0-7618-6436-3 (paperback : alk. paper)
eISBN: 978-0-7618-6437-0

The simplest explanation to Africa's problems is that it has never known good government.

Contents

Preface

Recently, I sat with an elderly Norwegian man during breakfast at a hotel. He was a director of an international non-governmental organization. He told me that he has spent most of his adult years as a development worker in Africa. In the course of our conversation, he narrated an interesting story of two countries: Zambia and Norway. For Zambia at independence in 1964, copper was driving its economy. It was the richest country in Africa second only to South Africa. At the same time, Norway was one of the poorest countries in Europe. Today Zambia is one of the poorest countries in the world, most of the people much poorer than they were at independence. On the other hand, Norway is one of the richest countries in Europe and in the world. In fact according to BBC World News of 5th January, 2013, Norway is the second best country for a child to be born in the world second only to Switzerland.

His explanation was that Zambia's copper enriched Americans and Europeans the same way it is enriching the Chinese today, and all this at the expense of the poor Zambian people. He said revenues from copper were used to subsidize consumption rather than to create investment in building a strong and sustainable economic base.

Norway discovered oil in the North Sea in the 1970s and used the revenue to enrich Norway and the Norwegian people. With this revenue, the national budget grew; and unlike Zambia, Norway put the money into good use—investing it in a national endowment fund. He told me that if the money in the fund were to be distributed, every Norwegian citizen would get at least $150,000 in cash. However, he was quick to point out that this would not be necessary because the state is functioning well, meeting its obligations towards its citizens. With a national endowment fund, a functioning state able to provide services and create an enabling environment for its citizens, the country takes care of its citizens today and even of those yet unborn.

From the two cases at our disposal, it is clear that the problem with Zambia (and it is the case with many countries in Africa) is not one of lack of resources but one of leadership, management and governance. The country with better leadership, management and governance like Norway will put its resources into better use with the primary goal of serving its citizens better. In short, the difference is in the 'government cultures' of the two countries.

The man told me that being over 70, he felt no need for being 'diplomatic' about hard facts and that he didn't have anything to lose by telling the truth. He went on to challenge me that as far as he could see, and from his experience of working as a development worker in Africa, he does not see Sub-Sahara Africa getting developed in the sense of lifting its millions of poor people out of poverty in my life time and in the life time of my children. The man went on to say, to my dismay, that unfortunate as it may sound, this continued underdevelopment of the masses on the continent works to the advantage of Europe, America, China, India and Brazil in that it offers them the opportunity to externalize Africa's resources with so much ease.

At the time of this conversation I had just turned forty. As a development practitioner, this was a very strong and disheartening statement. But soon after, I realized its probable truth when I read Marcus Garvey's biography, *A Negro with a Hat* by Colin Grant. In 1914, Marcus Garvey urged Africans to rise up and take their destiny in their own hands. He said,

> Sons and daughters of Africa, I say to you arise. Take on the toga of race pride and throw off the brand of ignominy which has kept you back for many centuries. Dash asunder the petty prejudices within your own fold; set at defiance the designation of 'nigger' uttered even by yourselves, and be Negro in the light of the Pharaohs of Egypt, Simons of Cyrene, Hannibals of Carthage . . . who have made, and are making history for the race, though depreciated and in many cases unwritten (Grant, 2009: 50).

Today, a century later, no significant shift has taken place among the close to one billion poor people on the continent. Or perhaps the major shift has been the change of oppressors, for the first were outsiders—slave traders, colonialists and imperialists. Today's oppressors are our own leaders; they came in the name of fighting the oppressors, but they soon turned out to be a deadly replacement.

The African situation is a gruesome state of affairs in need of an extreme remedy or response. Anything short of a values and systems revolution will not be sufficient to redirect the continent from its headlong journey into oblivion. A century has slipped through our fingers from the Marcus Garvey's revolutionary vision of a new Africa and another century may as well pass if no deep and revolutionary thinking and action assert themselves.

There is no question that Africa presents the worst case scenario of leadership failure, but it is also important to note that the subject is fast becoming one of the most significant problems on the globe, and all this despite the many case studies and literature on the subject. Willing disclosure of government (leadership) failure is rare even in mature democracies such as the United States and Europe, but it is worse in Africa where such a thing is just unheard of. In Africa, heads of state will blame anybody else except themselves for the problems facing their countries. If they run low of names on the list, they may go as far as blaming the Devil himself. The message of this book therefore applies to addressing the African leadership problem in particular and the global leadership problem in general.

I find a perfect allusion of Africa's dormancy and "stuckiness" to the story in George Orwell's *Animal Farm,* written in 1948. Since a problem known is a problem half-solved, perhaps there could be a formula for unlocking Africa's leadership malaise in this book.

CHAPTER 1: HITLER IS NOT DEAD

The central message of this book is that leadership improvement efforts in Africa fail because people focus more on changing or replacing individuals rather than the systems that the individuals inherit, create or maintain. Remove all bad leaders today but leave the system intact, count a few years, they will all be back, the only difference this time, they will be wearing new faces but with no positive change whatsoever. Robert Pirsig (quoted in Gilles and Alvarado, 2012:6) asserts that "if a revolution destroys a government, but the systemic patterns of thought that produced the government are left intact, then those patterns will repeat themselves. There is so much talk about the system. And so little understanding."

The essence of systems is captured well by Aime Cesaire (quoted in Biko, 1996: 82) in the mid-20th century when he observed,

> When I turn on my radio, when I hear that Negroes have been lynched in America, I say that I have been lied to: Hitler is not dead. When I turn on my radio and hear that in Africa, forced labor has been inaugurated and legislated, I say that we have certainly been lied to: Hitler is not dead.

Steve Biko (1996: 82), horrified by the "freedom" with which the apartheid system in South Africa was preying on human life, took a similar stance,

> When I turn on my radio, when I hear that someone in the Pondoland forest has been beaten and tortured, I say that we have been lied to: Hitler is not dead. When I turn on my radio, when I hear that someone in jail slipped off a piece of soap, fell and died I say that we have been lied to: Hitler is not dead, he is likely to be found in Pretoria.

Cesaire and Biko observed that although Adolf Hitler had died many years before, the system he left behind was well and alive; he did not need to be there in person for the system to function because the system was self-sustaining, with its own life, and not dependent on any individual. Removing Hitler did little to destroy the system. In that sense Hitler was not dead.

In describing the same apartheid regime in South Africa, Taylor (2012) observes:

> To the oppressed, the inhumane institutions and agencies of the previous white regime were experienced as a coherent and powerful system. Community activists strategized and plotted against 'the system.' The apartheid regime was experienced as one system of interrelated elements (or sub-systems) that as a whole had a devastating power over the lives of the majority of people. The term—'the system'—was a part of everyday language. When the security police appeared on the scene the warning would go out that 'the system' had arrived.

Systems create their own consciousness or memory to such an extent that they resemble seeds (Senge, 1990, Senge et al, 2004). Planting a seed will produce the same kind as the seed irrespective of the person who did the planting or who tends the garden today. Similarly, a system will naturally reproduce itself irrespective of the individual who is running it, or what name it is given. The solution is to plant a different seed or to consciously plant and tend a new system.

A good garden can be overrun by weeds if left untended; a good system can be overrun by "weeds," in the process churning initially good leaders into bad ones. Incidents of initially good leaders who have turned against their people to become the people's oppressors and steal from them are not rare on the continent. A loss of vigilant consciousness among the followers and leaders leads to mutation and thereby good systems turn into dangerous machines. The responsibility of nurturing good systems is the responsibility of leadership. "Leadership" in this case does not only mean individual leaders but also the followers, for effective leadership are the matured, healthy interaction between leaders and followers. James Allen, in his classic book, *As a Man Thinketh,* written over a hundred years ago rightly observed when he said,

> It has been usual for men to think and to say, many men are slaves because one is an oppressor; let us hate the oppressor. Now, however, there is among an increasing few a tendency to reverse this judgment, and to say that one man is an oppressor because many are slaves; let us despise the slaves. The truth is that the oppressor and the slave are cooperators in ignorance, and while seeming to afflict each other, are in reality afflicting themselves.

Inspired by the writings of and about Martin Luther King, Jr., this book discusses leadership and governance experiences in Africa since independence. Martin Luther King Jr., leader of the American civil rights revolution of the 1960s lived in a period when there was a huge gap between America's ideal of a democratic society and its reality. Today many African countries find themselves in the same situation. They have accepted the body of democracy but they are still struggling to embrace its spirit.

Martin Luther King Jr., spent his life helping the nation to identify, expose and confront its contradictions in its practice of democracy. He recognized the problem for what it was: not some individuals or white people but an evil system called segregation. The problem could not be solved by changing or replacing individuals or fighting white people but withdrawing cooperation from the evil system and fighting for its replacement with a better system. The persistent and endemic problems Africa continues to face irrespective of who succeeds who in state houses is evidence that the problems are more systemic in nature and hence the need to target the systems more than the individuals therein.

Martin Luther King's message on how to break evil systems in essence was: help the poor come to a conviction that some things are wrong and unacceptable at any cost and that some things are right and worthy fighting for and if necessary dying for. In other words, help the poor reject and not adjust to unjust systems. The poor masses must be told who they are—that they are citizens with rights and privileges that the state is obliged to provide, and that if the state fails to do so the grassroots people have power to remove that government using peaceful means and replace it with a more capable one. In addition, the people must be told what they can aspire to—that they have every right to aspire to be the best and to have the best just as anyone else in the world, and no one should tell them or convince them otherwise. They have a right to put in their best effort for individual and collective progress and the state has the responsibility to provide an enabling environment for them to realize their dreams. No one should tell the people that nature has destined them to be victims of poverty and that they should accept it as a fact. People must be told emphatically that poverty is a social construction and not a natural or divine order. Lastly, the grassroots people must be given the means to employ in pursuing their aspirations and in dealing with forces or anyone who stands in their way to achieve their legitimate aspirations (Carson, 1991, Phillips, 1998, Washinton, 1998).

Since the interaction between citizens and their governments or the state is the most visible practice of leadership in a country, this book will concentrate on this relationship to illustrate the primacy of systems over individual leaders or single regimes. The insights will apply to all situations bemoaning leadership. The message of the book is not a call to overthrow legitimate governments, but a call to give apparently ossified, unresponsive, unaccountable and uncaring governments enough and unrelenting pressure so that the unjust systems inherent in them can be overhauled and replaced with more empowering and genuinely democratic ones.

The most common characteristic of unjust systems is poor leadership. The Mo Ibrahim Award, the biggest award in the world aimed at encouraging good leadership among African Presidents with annual prize money of $5 million initial payment and thereafter $200,000 per year for life for the recipient could not find any winner in 2009 and 2010. This is a grave reflection of the leadership situation on the continent.

The obvious battle in Africa today is the war against poverty prolonged, not by the lack of resources, but by the lack of vision in most governments, leaders' inability to learn from history, and inability to adhere to basic morals and ethics befitting leaders. In short, if Africa is being written off the developmental map of the world today, it is all thanks to bad leadership. Africa is increasingly being conceptualized as an area of darkness, the source of danger, chaos and risk to other parts of the world (Menzel, 1996: 86) and primarily, because of bad leadership. This statement is being written with full recognition of the relative progress the continent has generally made in some aspects of leadership and governance over the past few years. We have made some progress in holding regular elections and establishing some democratic institutions. The fact that I can write a book of this nature without fear of (physical) harm or "disappearing" as it used to happen in the past is also proof that some progress has been made. Too few Africans have written about leadership in their countries and on the continent because of fear. Many of those who tried were persecuted, jailed or even killed. Despite this progress however, as far as listening to and meeting the needs of ordinary citizens is concerned, Africa is still in a big crisis. Masses of poor people are sliding back to dark ages pushed by the irresponsible decisions and actions of their leaders.

We have come to realize that in Africa, just as in many parts of the world, governments have a tendency to become corrupt unless they are given sustained pressure by the citizenry. If governments have no fear of their citizens, they have a tendency to grow monstrous. A key developmental task therefore is the education of the masses to understand their interests as well as their organization and mobilization so that they are able to act at all times, in the defense of those interests. In this way, the masses would not allow those who seek to dominate and usurp power from them and place it in their own hands to take advantage (Mbeki, 2000: 146).

In the book, I use the *Animal Farm* story as a model to reflect on the real and lived leadership and governance experience of many African countries since independence. By comparing the story of animal farm and the real experiences of a few countries on the continent I aim to show that many African countries are 'animal farm systems' in need of serious changes or complete overhaul of systems.

This book is coming at a time when the world is experiencing an unprecedented uprising in which the citizenry is migrating from the peripheral to the centre of action as far as shaping the destiny of their generations, nations and countries is concerned. This reversal is redefining power relations between the state and the citizens with shifts in favor of the citizens. Sub-Saharan Africa remains the world's most formidable development challenge and it is yet to rise up to the current awakening of consciousness. In many Sub-Saharan countries today citizen space continues to shrink while poverty and governance conditions continue to slide towards intolerable and unbearable levels. This is creating perfect prerequisites for the region to rise up and join the rest of the world in the struggle for genuine citizenship.

This book aims to be a catalyst for this timely and historical structural change process upon which the hope for a fairer world is based, for abuse can only prevail when citizens are dispossessed of their power. Using Martin Luther King Jr.'s "model," and observations from the Arab revolution of the second decade of the 21st century, I make some suggestions on how poor grassroots people can exercise more leadership by organizing and mobilizing to break animal farm systems in their countries.

The primary responsibility for challenging and uprooting animal farm systems in Africa lies squarely on the shoulders of the youths. History is thrusting on young people of Africa a critical challenge to complete the liberation and democratic process in the interest of the poor grassroots people. To date only a handful of countries on the continent have shown real seriousness to make this a reality hence the need to knock the youths and the grassroots out of slumber, fatalism, apathy and complacency to a new level of consciousness and vigilance. The grassroots, more especially young people must be challenged to refuse, resist and repudiate animal farm systems.

How young people of Sub-Sahara Africa will deal with this challenge will show the world whether they are serious about taking their leadership role and getting the respect as a serious group of people or whether they should still be treated as children unable to tell their right from their left. Developing and practicing political consciousness is the prelude to good governance and ultimately genuine sustainable development, which is in the interest of the people at the grassroots level.

Fighting the old oppressive systems which masquerade as democratic systems when in reality they are dictatorships, and replacing them with empowering systems that practice genuine democracy and good governance is the next struggle for Sub-Saharan Africa. And this calls for the same magnitude of effort and even more as in the era of the struggle for independence against the colonial system.

It will come as a surprise to many that the civil rights student movement in the 1960s in America was influenced by the liberation struggle in Africa against the colonial system. In the words of Martin Luther King, Jr., (Carson, 1998: 139),

> The liberation struggle in Africa was the great single international influence on American Negro students. Frequently, I heard them say that if their African brothers could break the bonds of colonialism, surely America could break Jim Crow.

In the 1990s we were asking what lessons the Middle East can learn from Sub-Saharan Africa after the democratic wind of change had blown across the region, showing the exit door to the likes of Zambia's Kenneth Kaunda and Malawi's Kamuzu Banda.

Today, roles have reversed; today the new generation of Africans will learn from their African American brothers and sisters on how they broke Jim Crow, and how the people of Tunisia, Libya and Egypt undid the shackles of bondage. Africa is a case of a people who have forgotten their past. They have forgotten who they were, what they achieved and what means they employed to accomplish them. In many cases, these are not properly recorded, they are not in school curricula, and now we have to learn from people who were influenced by us. We managed to fight and send the colonialists running, but now we are complacent if not impotent before obvious recalcitrant animal farm systems.

The animal farm systems are a formidable front because unlike the individuals in colonial systems who were able to recognize the "wind of change" and eventually left the continent, many of the outstanding animal farm systems today are, in the words of Martin Luther King, made up of "old guards who would rather die than surrender" (Phillips, 1998). This makes calls for persistent effort and will to do the job—uprooting deep-rooted animal farm systems- such a significant and urgent message. The job to clean Africa of its animal farm systems is not for the timid; it is the job for those with that porcupine cover.

Fear is a key obstacle to surmount. The great tragedy in Africa today is not the powerlessness of the grassroots but the silence of the enlightened and educated people who are paralyzed by fear. People must conquer fear to liberate themselves.

The question of fear must be dealt with by each individual who wants to enlist in the army of change agents. Counting the cost is part and parcel of the game. There will be consequences and willing to face them is a measure of how serious one is about their convictions. If one is filled with fear, they cannot stand up against animal farm systems. In the same vein, if one has too many attachments the cost of losing them may be too much. This is why most of the individuals who have brought about significant political change in this world started young when they had the confidence of youth and without many attachments. During the Arab Spring in Egypt, it was after the people there had overcome the deeply entrenched fear of the police force, which exceeded 1.7 million, that they finally rose up, forcing a deeply entrenched authoritarian regime to come tumbling down.

Greg Mills (2010) makes a bold assertion that Africa's people are poor because their leaders have made this choice. In this book, I extend the assertion by stating that African poor masses have the right to reject this choice and I strive to show how they can do it. My goal is to state frankly what everyone already knows.

The next chapter starts with a reflection and observations on some of the African countries I have visited.

CHAPTER 2: A "SNAPSHOT" OF AFRICA

Nigeria

I arrived in Nigeria for the first time on 2nd October, 2010 about 10.00 a.m. Contrary to the many stories I had heard about Nigerian migration, the migration/passport control procedures went very smoothly and efficiently. Within twenty minutes we were all cleared and we had collected our luggage. I had planned to spend only five days in Nigeria but the passport officer generously stamped additional 25 days, joking that five days were too short for me to find a Nigerian girlfriend. "I am already married," I told him. "And what does being married have to do with getting a girlfriend?" was his reply.

We needed to change some money. My Nigerian friend told me it was better to change the money at the black market because the official rates were too low. All this while, boys and taxi drivers swarmed us looking for business to pick us up to the local airport on the other side of the international airport as I was supposed to connect from the local airport in Lagos to Abuja in the afternoon. He told me he had in mind one makeshift mosque as he trusted the Muslim black market money changers more than the other boys because, "the Muslims seemed to be more serious with their religion," he said. He was quick however to point out that his observation mostly applied among small businesses or petty business owners and that he was not sure if those doing big business or real business, as he called it, adhered to the same "code of conduct."

Later, a driver took us to the local airport. It was while on our way to this airport that I learnt from the driver about a bomb that had gone off on a road in Abuja the previous day. It went off a few minutes after the President had passed the spot; the President was going to grace the 50th year independence celebration for the country. Apparently he was the target of the bomb blast, but for some reason, Providence perhaps, he narrowly missed it or it narrowly missed him. Twelve people died and many sustained serious injuries.

My friend left me at the airport as he was from Lagos. Before he did, he asked me if I had "prepared enough" to proceed to Abuja. I didn't quite understand the question but after he had clarified it, I understood the concern: whether I had enough money for my expenses in Abuja. "Yes," I said. "I have a credit card."

"Then we'll have to make quick arrangements to cancel the hotel booking in Abuja," he said.

When I asked why, he told me the hotel and many like it do not accept credit cards.

He coordinated with someone in Abuja to change my hotel booking and he told me that the hotels that accept credit cards would normally charge more than twice the rate of the hotel I was booked at. Matters were complicated because I could not use the ATM machines as I had messed up my password.

My flight to Abuja was at 3.00 p.m. I arrived in time when another flight to Abuja was just boarding. I asked if I could be put on that one. They tried and later said something to the effect that it was not possible for some reason. I couldn't understand why I could not be put on that flight which was obviously not full. I got back my tickets and went on to wait. Later, I learnt that there had been some changes: we were supposed to board a 3.10 p.m. but we would now board a 3.30 p.m. When we got into the plane, over the intercom, the pilot announced that a government official, a governor, was leaving and soon after another one would be arriving so the "airport was temporarily closed." We were told we would have to wait until he was given permission to leave. We ended up waiting for two hours in the plane. I sent a text message to the person who would be waiting for me in Abuja to let them know that I would be arriving late but I did not get a response.

When we finally left, I kept wondering what was awaiting me in Abuja. My intuitive apprehension about Abuja proved right. We landed in Abuja at 6.15 p.m. The taxi driver had been waiting for me from 3.00 p.m. I couldn't understand because 3.00 p.m. was the time I was supposed to leave Lagos. He was tired and irritated. We drove to town—a distance of 50 kilometers. The driver and his colleague, who was a worker at the hotel I had been previously booked into, explained to me how the President had narrowly escaped death the previous day.

Since the hotel I was booked in could not accept credit cards and apparently no alternative arrangement had been made as I thought, we went straight looking for other hotels. We went to the first hotel. They said, yes they could accept credit cards but the rates were just too high for me. We went to Sheraton hotel. Their rates were even higher. We went to a third hotel. This one looked better than the original hotel I was booked to and their rates were half those of my original hotel but they too could not accept credit cards.

It was getting late and I was getting more and more apprehensive. Meanwhile with all the rounds we were making, the taxi bill was skyrocketing. We went to the last hotel. It was a big, high class hotel with reasonable rates and yes, they could accept credit cards. We quickly did the paper work and it was time for me to pay a deposit before getting the keys to my room. I handed my visa card to the cashier and then for the first time and to my surprise the machine gave a 'no' answer after he swiped my card. I was surprised. I did not know what this meant. I had just used the card to settle my bills in the morning on the same day in Dar es Salaam. He explained to me that my card was blocked and to unblock it I was supposed to call a bank. He explained to me that this was a security measure against corruption which he said was very rampant in Nigeria. This was Saturday night and all the banks were closed. I had now come to the end of the road and I was getting very desperate.

The driver's friend, who was an employee at the original hotel I was booked to proved to be the angel of the night. He called me aside and suggested that we go back to the original hotel and said we could talk things through as we drove back. To cut a long story short, out of desperation in a strange land, we passed by a "black market" and I changed all the little cash I had and then planned how I was going to survive the five days I had planned to spend in Nigeria. I now went into survival mode and I had to prioritize. First on my list was to pay for my accommodation, second was to have enough money for a taxi to take me back to the airport when the five days were over. Then I had to make a choice between eating and paying for a taxi to take me around Abuja to do the work I had come for. I chose to work rather than eat. I went on an involuntary fast—starvation. For the first time in a long time I felt hungry and I was able differentiate between hunger and appetite.

My guide showed up on Monday at 10.00 a.m. and advised me that we could save the transport money by using public transport and tricycles rather than the normal taxis. That proved to be a wise idea and I managed to save enough money for a light lunch and supper which I bought from some street women which I really appreciated. Meanwhile, my angel friend, Mr. Benson, had offered to buy supper for me. He said he could have the amount deducted from his salary. I was too embarrassed to accept and I politely declined. In the morning of Wednesday, we worked out the bills and costs—by the way taxis in Abuja and especially the tricycles do not issue receipts so we had to be very creative.

Mr. Benson organized the taxi to get me to the airport. He even came along to leave me at the airport. On the way he asked me about Malawi, my country: "Is it a rich country? Are the people good? What is its population? Why are there only 14 million people when Lagos alone has 20 million?"

In turn I asked him for his e-mail address so that I should drop him a note when I arrived home. "I don't have an e-mail address," he told me. As I got out of the taxi, Mr. Benson's cell phone rang. It was his boss. He was asking where he was and that his presence was needed immediately at the office. I quickly paid the driver and they left immediately. There was no time for proper good byes and proper closure. I wondered at the irony of it all. Was this the way to say good bye to an angel?

As we were getting to the bus that took us to the plane, I couldn't believe my eyes when I saw the first President of Zambia, Kenneth Kaunda. Abuja of all the places! I made it a point to greet him with a handshake and introduce myself to him though I knew it would probably not mean much to him but to me it would. What surprised me more was the absence of pomp around him. He did not seem to have any private security and most people did not seem to recognize or know him. Probably he was too far away from home and of course, he was from another generation.

As we flew from Abuja to Lagos, I reflected on the two main observations I had made in Nigeria. One was the preoccupation with titles and the other was what I could call, "extreme assertiveness bordering on aggressiveness." Preoccupation with titles was perhaps the greatest impression I had about Nigeria. I saw and heard of Chiefs, *Ogas*, *Otumbas*, Al hadjis, *Igwes*, Doctors, Professors, Sirs (I kept wondering where they were knighted), Engineers, Barristers and many more others. It seemed to me that some individuals had stopped taking titles such as Dr. and Professor as academic ranks, now turning them into a source of commanding respect in society especially in politics. Some individuals had up to five earned PhDs. I had a similar feeling in Tanzania when I saw so many professors, lawyers and doctors running for parliamentary seats.

Are they all motivated by a genuine need to serve in politics? Where are professors, doctors or engineers better situated to make a contribution or to serve the society? Is it in politics or in their respective fields?

The guide who took me around in Abuja told me that in Nigeria you cannot afford to be "soft like those East Africans." She said, "There they speak slowly, they walk slowly and they are too respectful. If you are like that in Nigeria, your life will be short as people will 'crowd and squeeze you out.'" She finished with a warning of some kind: "Nigeria is tough."

The flight from Abuja to Lagos was very turbulent as it was very cloudy. Two women sitting across the isle held hands and began to pray fervently asking God for "protection of the plane." The pilot announced that the turbulence was normal but the women did not stop. The person next to me said, "Do not be surprised. They are not extremists. In Nigeria planes do fall out of the sky."

When we landed in Lagos at the local airport, I went to the taxi rank to get a taxi to the international airport. "2000 Naira," the gentleman told me. "No, but I paid 1500 Naira when I was coming this way."

"Ok, 1500 Naira," he said as he lifted my bag into the back of the car. I then realized he was not the driver. He was rather a kind of coordinator for the drivers. He called for a driver and gave him instructions, "Pick the gentleman to the international airport at 1500 Naira but he will pay the gate fee of 300 Naira as well." Before I could protest, the car had started off, and soon was at full speed.

I was so tired and did not have any more energy for another fight. I gave the driver four five hundred Naira notes. I was expecting my change of 200 Naira after paying at the gate. As I was disembarking, the driver told me he only had five hundred Naira notes and therefore could not give me my change of 200 Naira. The total amount of money I paid therefore came back to 2000 Naira, and not 1500 as I had originally negotiated for and agreed with that gentleman.

On the check-in queue I met a lady lawyer from Malawi now based in Namibia. She told me she was coming from a church, Synagogue Church of All Nations led by Prophet T.B. Joshua. She told me she had been there for a week for a personal spiritual retreat. She showed me several of her colleagues from different countries that were there for similar reasons. They had come to the airport straight from the church under police escort to ensure their security and to cut through traffic jam. "That is how seriously government takes some churches here," she told me.

Finally, the plane left at 11 p.m. I heaved a sigh of relief. I had survived Nigeria.

While improving in relative terms, talking to ordinary citizens on the street, one is left with the feeling that Nigeria has generally remained the same. Reading Chinua Achebe's, *The Trouble with Nigeria* (1983) one is left with the feeling that the issues Achebe discussed in 1983 still persist and most of them refuse to go away. Tribalism, "a false image of ourselves," social injustice and a cult of mediocrity, indiscipline, corruption remain largely impervious. While Nigeria is already the most populous country in Africa (one out of every four

Africans is a Nigerian), today it stands on the verge of a run-away population explosion. According to the BBC News of 5th January, 2013, from a survey of 150 countries, Nigeria is the worst place for a child to be born in.

Nigeria still stuns the world by being the sixth producer of oil in the world and yet most of the time its own filling stations are dry. Nigeria has to deal with the amnesty program for the Nigerian militants in the Niger Delta. In the words of an ex-militant, "They (the government) told us we should leave the creeks for peace and we have come out. But government is not doing what they promised us. Only those in the big, big camps are benefiting but if we fight back now they will say we want to make trouble" (Mbah, 2011: 27).

A major explanation is that while Nigeria has changed over time it has changed leaders but not the system. As I left Nigeria, there was a lot of excitement especially among the young people about the elections which they all knew would usher in President Goodluck Jonathan. They said he represented change and with him the prospects were high for Nigeria. The older people were less excited. Perhaps time and experience had taught them more. When President Jonathan won the elections I was excited in solidarity with the young people. But I wondered if he was just another leader or someone who would deal with the system for genuine change.

Zambia

From Nigeria, I went to Zambia. Zambia was much easier to handle. I was more prepared after my lessons in Nigeria, and in addition, most of the basic systems in Zambia seem to work.

In Zambia I stayed at a Protea Hotel next to the late former President Frederick Chiluba's building which he had planned to make into the Frederick Chiluba Centre for Democracy, a project that was never to be because he was caught up in some serious corruption scandal. "Do you know Mr Chiluba?" the driver asked me as we were passing by the building. Before I replied, he shot another: "Do you know the court in the UK found him guilty of stealing many millions of US dollars, but surprisingly a Zambian court said he was not guilty of any charges? Do you want to tell me the court in the UK was wrong?" He said many people in Zambia felt it was the Zambian court which was in the wrong.

During the last meeting with my host in Zambia, he told me he had just visited the website for the Zambian Parliament which posts the CVs for the parliamentarians. He said what was most outstanding to him was the observation that the highest qualifications for most of the MPs was O level or four years secondary school examination level; and that the most prominent occupation of the MPs was indicated as "businessman" or "businesswoman." He wondered what type of businesses they did before they became MPs and more so how such a group of people can provide strategic direction and leadership to a nation in the 21st Century. "Where are the graduates?" he wondered. "No wonder our country does not seem to be making any strides," he said.

I was a little bit surprised because in my own country, a good percentage of the MPs were doctors, professors, lawyers and professionals in general. What a contrast! But were these professionals able to provide strategic leadership to the country in a relatively and significantly different way from their counterparts in Zambia? I am afraid no.

There are a lot of puppet PhDs and Professors in politics today. Instead of being agents of change in their political parties, they have been swallowed up by the system. They leave their intelligence behind to practice brainless politics. This poses a lot of questions whether there is indeed a correlation between higher learning and its value on one hand and power to provide practical solutions to peoples' every day challenges on the other. These are people who are supposed to provide guidance and critique, but for selfish and myopic reasons, they allow themselves to pay blind loyalty to often less educated or misguided leaders. They would rather succumb to brainless politics than lose the opulent life styles politics accords them from money meant for the poor masses. They live in air conditioned houses when the poor sleep in squalor; they have scandalously big swimming pools when the poor can hardly afford clean drinking water. They can never suffer to lose membership to clubs where they get free drinks at the expense of the poor masses; and (that) luxury of globetrotting (Onyeani, 2000: 100).

Whenever I see so many professionals leave their fields of expertise to become MPs, I stop in my tracks. For sure we need more "strategic people" in parliament but where is a medical doctor better situated, in parliament or in hospital? Where is a professor better situated, in parliament or at the university? Are they all 'called' to politics? What is their motivation? Perhaps they believe that the only place one can exercise power and influence in Africa is in politics as the space in other avenues such as business, higher centers of learning, and religion are very limited and not as rewarding as politics. Politicians are among the richest and most admired category of people in Africa.

What makes a good politician or Member of Parliament? What are the critical qualifications of an MP? For me, I think to be an effective MP requires three main qualifications. These are legitimacy, relevance and sustainability. Legitimacy means that the MP must be connected with the people at values, affective or transformational level. This means he or she must be the personification of the values of the people. Relevance means he or she must understand the needs of the people and become their advocate. Sustainability means he or she must be able to influence and thereby bring about change, visible and lasting change for the better to his or her constituency. These requirements are not saying anything about academic qualifications.

When we look at leaders like Martin Luther King, Jr. and Malcom X, we observe that Martin Luther King, Jr. had high academic qualifications. He had a doctorate degree. Malcolm X had no formal academic qualifications. Both leaders however were impactful at a global level in their own way. The fact that we still talk about them today is part of the evidence of their impact. They left a challenge to the world to create an ideal society, a mission we are still struggling to fulfill today. One thing that is common about the two men though is that they were self-made individuals characterized by a grand vision of a changed society and personal hard work to develop themselves to rise up through conscious action to the level of their visions. This puts a level ground between academically and unacademically trained leaders. Obviously, academically trained leaders may have some advantages over the academically untrained leaders but a fact of life is that not everyone who is academically trained has enough consciousness about these matters.

For MPs to provide strategic leadership in a country, what is needed is not whether they are academically educated or not but whether they have legitimacy, relevance and sustainability. This said, however, I believe that a minimum of a genuine first degree would form a good foundation for one to lead at a national level in the modern world. The good news is, with so many educational opportunities around one who truly aspires national leadership can easily acquire this qualification.

Again, we see that effectiveness does not depend on whether one is "educated" or not but whether the system allows and empowers people to develop themselves and make their contribution. Change efforts in Africa must focus more on changing systems so that the systems can deliver the required ends rather than being preoccupied with changing individuals, leaving the systems intact.

Ghana

In May 2009, I had the opportunity to visit Accra, Ghana on an assignment to conduct a leadership development seminar. The last time I was in Ghana was 2007. It was wonderful to be back in Accra. Accra is a big, beautiful and impressive African city. Ghana is the first country to gain independence in Africa from the British colonial rule in 1957 and today it is held by many as a model of democracy in Africa.

When I go to any city one thing I make sure to do is to find enough time to go where the "real people and the life are." Although my schedule is usually tight with business engagements, I usually find time to visit the markets, villages, streets and social places in the nights. That is where real life is. If one leaves a country without visiting these places, they will usually leave a country with a wrong impression. I have observed that hotels are the same everywhere. There is no difference whether you are in Washington D.C. or Maputo. If you leave a country without getting out of the hotel you may think all the countries are the same.

Ghana was then just four months into a new government. The ruling party lost and the opposition came into government. Except for the fact that I knew about it, there was almost no way of knowing that the country had just undergone a general election. Of course a few posters were still hanging in town as a reminder. Ghana is a model of peaceful elections—a rare contrast to Kenya, Ivory Coast and Zimbabwe.

At the market, the women and men were as friendly as usual with that African smile unique to the continent. Although I don't understand and speak the local language Twi, I could feel as deeply connected to the people as my own which of course they are.

One major difference I noticed was that the electricity blackouts I found in 2007 had vanished. In 2007, there were 12 hours of blackout everyday—literally everyday. This time, I did not experience any blackout and I was very surprised. I asked a Ghanaian friend what had happened. He told me that in 2007 the river that provided hydro-electric power had dried up because of a drought. The drought had ended and that's why the blackouts had vanished. I was happy that the blackouts were gone but I was worried that the root cause of the problem had not been dealt with. In this era of climate change, there is no guarantee that the droughts will not come again. Thinking about the proverb *if you cut a piece of a liana creeper without removing the roots, it will continue to creep*, I left Ghana wondering if the new government had begun to ask the right questions on this issue.

Southern Sudan

In May, 2010, I had the opportunity to travel to Juba, Southern Sudan. As the plane descended towards the airport, the first scene was the vast fleet of United Nations (UN) vehicles and planes, a reminder of the conflict, the 22-year long war between the South and the North, the country had just come from and the uncertainty of the situation at the moment. The airport is one of the most basic I have ever seen but surprisingly very efficient. We were out of the airport within 10 minutes.

As we drove to the hotel, it became immediately clear to me that Southern Sudan and Northern Sudan are very different and to think that they were one country is almost inconceivable. No two places can be so different in terms of levels of economic and infrastructural development, climate, culture and religion. This has been long recognized and a Comprehensive Peace Agreement was signed some years before which ultimately led to a referendum in January 2011 for the people of Southern Sudan to decide whether to remain part of the North or to become a different or new country. As we walked on the streets of Juba, the excitement and expectation to become a new country was palpable and almost tangible. The vote was cast and decided in favor of separation by a whooping 99 percent.

We took some time to visit Konyokonyo market, one of the biggest markets in Juba. Most of the traders there are Ugandan and Congolese. In fact, Uganda is the lifeline of Juba and most parts of Southern Sudan. All the basic things come from there. A friend told me that there is no food in some parts of North Uganda because it is all sold to Southern Sudan at very lucrative prices. Most of the hotels are managed by Ethiopians. The waitresses are mostly Kenyan, Ugandan, Eritrean or Ethiopian.

As we walked through the campus of the University of Juba, it was very clear that the University, like many in Africa, was not designed to produce women and men who can take on national political and economic leadership—the two key pillars for national self-determination. We were told that all the strategic faculties are in the North.

Lastly, we visited the grave of the fallen leader, John Garang where I knelt down and said a wish. My wish was that God should give Africa more leaders like him—leaders who are selfless and are willing to lay down their lives for their countries. The shadow of John Garang still looms large. He is still seen as the great unifying factor among the diverse peoples of Southern Sudan. His mysterious death added to his already larger-than-life image.

As the plane lifted from Juba Airport, I looked down and wondered about Southern Sudan as a country about to be born in a few months' time. Its leaders know what most countries in Africa have become after independence. A good number of them are worse off than they were under colonial rule mostly because of the development models and leadership styles they chose. The slate of Southern Sudan was clean and unwritten. What story of development were they going to write on it? What route of development and leadership are they going to take? Are they going to follow the conventional way or will they show Africa a new and better alternative?

Tanzania

September and October, 2010 were very busy months. An assignment took me to Kenya, Tanzania, Nigeria, Botswana, Zambia and finally Mombasa, Kenya. Traveling across the countries and cities gave me an opportunity to see new places, revisit old places and also to take a general time for developmental reflection. One of my places of great interest was Dar es Salaam, Tanzania.

I arrived at Julius Nyerere International Airport with a colleague from Nigeria. Our hotel was about 45 km away from the airport on the shores of Indian Ocean. The distance from the airport to the hotel gave us an opportunity to drive through town from one side to the other. I was half asleep throughout the drive. But when we arrived at the hotel my Nigerian friend asked me a question which I found to be very interesting. He asked, "Who was that man we have been seeing on the billboards literally every thirty seconds since we left the airport; surely he must be a great musician, entertainer or something?" I told him, he was the President of Tanzania and what he saw were campaign billboards. He was seeking a re-election? He then asked me, "Where then are his opponents?" We did not see a single billboard of any other contestant. Somebody who overheard our conversation joined in and told us there are seven contestants for the presidency including the President but we could not see the other contestants because "they have posters." We did not understand this, upon further inquiry, he explained that the opposition candidates cannot afford the billboards and as a substitute they use black and white A4 photocopied posters which are posted on trees. We could not see these because we were driving in a car, he told us. He himself did not seem to have any problem with this.

Susain Geiger argues that the nationalist identity left by the Julius Nyerere leadership was strong enough to survive the first 30 years with many achievements in real economic growth and a better life quality for all. The key question is: "How much is left of that sense of pride of being Tanzanian and in being an African people?" Mbilinyi (in Chachange and Cassam, 2010:85) gives a contrast by presenting Tanzania's (and indeed most of Africa's) modern day reality: "What do we have today? Horrendous gaps between the rich and the poor, the powerful and the powerless, with wealth and power being openly flaunted in the faces of the excluded majority."

In less than ten years Tanzania has witnessed the "mallization" of its society and economy. Shopping centers spring up with fences, gates and guards to lock out the poor majority. An increasing number of the wealthy and the powerful now live in gated communities—also protected by fences guards and dogs—and thus Tanzanian society begins to resemble that of apartheid South Africa, a system which its leaders once sought to demolish. Rich children attend elite private schools, while the poor majority attends low quality government and private schools that resemble superficially, the old "native" schools for Africans of the colonial period. I say superficially because those colonial native schools did at least teach their students how to read and write, whereas today many primary school leavers remain functionally illiterate.

As I left Tanzania, I couldn't stop wondering if it is really true that democracy is taking root in Africa and whether the people really have the freedom to choose the leaders they want. I also kept wondering what it will take to shift power from the hands of the ruling party politicians to the hands of ordinary citizens in Africa. Most Importantly, I also wondered whether an opposition party will ever rule Tanzania and what it will take to make that happen. This reminded me of Robert Mugabe's famous question, "How can a political party in power lose an election?"

Malawi

I recently went to collect our car from a service mechanic at a garage together with my wife. When we arrived, the mechanic asked us to give him some thirty minutes so that he could do final touches on the car. I knew that meant at least one hour of waiting so instead of sitting down and getting bored with waiting, we decided to take a walk. After walking for some time, we decided to buy a drink and rest in grocery because it was getting too dark as there was yet another electricity blackout. At least there were some candles in the grocery.

After a short while, we got into a conversation on leadership with the grocer. He began talking about the frequency of blackouts and said as a man in his late sixty's he is very worried about the future of the country and the continent as a whole; and more importantly that of my generation and our children. He wondered if anybody really cares about the future of Africa. His biggest disappointment was that everyone seems to have adjusted to and normalized mediocrity—for example—people now think that electricity blackouts are normal, long queues at fuel stations and water taps that don't run are normal.

I interjected and suggested that the failure of leadership could be because young people are not given a chance to bring in new thinking—it's the same old people who are clinging to power and closing out young people and new ideas. He looked at me and laughed. He convincingly showed me that new young leaders who have been tried or given a chance have not shown any difference. He pointed to me a few young and "brilliant" civil society organization leaders, ministers and even presidents who have not demonstrated any difference from the "old guard." He said, "If you look at the way parliaments and political parties behave you will see that there is no difference between those that went to school and those that did not. There is no difference between professors and 'illiterates.' There is no difference between the old and the young." The biggest challenge, he added, was that today, Africa and indeed the whole world is lacking individuals who are critical and independent and are willing to go against the system no matter the cost—individuals who are willing to do the right thing no matter the sacrifice. These are individuals who are true leaders and not just rulers. We have too many rulers and too few leaders.

"Today Africa is experiencing an unprecedented growth but most of the growth is externally driven mostly from China. With more infrastructural growth, without investment in electricity and water supply, we should expect more water shortages and electricity blackouts for ordinary citizens." To him, this will undermine the growth and make it unsustainable. "Leadership is first and foremost about people and providing their basic needs like electricity and water, and as long as we don't have leaders we should forget about real development," he told us.

"Leadership begins as personal responsibility," he added. "What are you and your wife personally going to do to exercise this responsibility in ensuring that your house and community have electricity and running water all day all night as you very well know that this is your right?" the grocer asked us. As I was thinking about an answer, I looked at my watch and it was time to go for the vehicle.

It is very expensive to be poor. Recently I was invited to be part of an African thought leaders meeting on what African rooted and African driven development would look like. This meeting took place in Bellagio, Italy. It was convened and sponsored by the Rockefeller Foundation.

To travel to Italy from Malawi one can only get the visa from Lusaka, Zambia, and one has to go to the Italian embassy in Zambia in person to be interviewed. I traveled to Lusaka on a Sunday and I had to stay in Zambia until a Friday to wait for the visa. There was no direct flight between Blantyre and Lusaka which normally takes 50 minutes. I had to travel by air to Johannesburg and then to Lusaka. A trip which took me about 12 hours! On top of the flight expenses, my sponsors had to keep me in an expensive hotel for a full week just to get a visa. That year alone, I cancelled another trip to Italy and two to the Netherlands because of visa complications as one cannot get these from Malawi.

The point I am trying to raise is that it is very expensive to be poor or to come from a country that does not have the capacity to have the strategic embassies important for geopolitical significance. I empathized with my sponsors because the situation of my country, the impossibility to get visas from within the country, makes one "heavy to carry." It is no wonder that many African countries, for their logistical inconveniences, get passed by and left behind especially when there are better options elsewhere.

When young people are trying to make a developmental contribution to their countries and to the continent, it is very frustrating if their governments cannot provide a supportive and conducive environment. While prioritizing addressing the basic needs of the poor masses, it is also very important to remember that geopolitical strategic positioning is crucial for national success. Creative and innovative young people need to be supported by their governments to play on the global stage.

Conclusion

Visiting villages and rural areas in Africa, I have always been surprised by how more similar than different they are. There are very few villages or rural areas on the continent where people are satisfied with the performance of their governments. The story is the same in most countries: inadequate infrastructure, poor facilities and service provision and soaring costs of living. Added to this are MPs who appear around election times only to abandon them after winning to resurface at the time of the next elections. The people know what a good MP should be and should do but owing to high levels of poverty they are forced to sacrifice principles at the altar of survival by choosing the bad but rich MP who gives them "sweets" during election times to coax them to vote for him or her. Merit and performance are rarely considered in the big picture.

In urban areas one sees swelling numbers of unemployed youth who spend hours idling and loitering in town. They often survive on the mirage of government promises of some youth development programs that rarely come to reality and if it does only those who are "connected" benefit.

Then there is a handful few whose opulence ascendancy knows no bounds. Leading this pack are politicians, mostly of the ruling party and a few individuals who are "connected." This is against a background of Africa being a continent of close to one billion but with only one percent contribution to world trade.

Then there are few "middle class" graduates and business people who are generally comfortable and their general attitude is, "If it is ok with me, my wife/husband and two children, that is enough and I should not rock the boat." These people rarely interact with the rural masses or the suffering urban youth and can hardly identify and empathize with them. A good number of them are more familiar with European and American cities and ways of life than their own villages and ways of life.

For most Africans life has remained the same over the last two thousand years. The only difference being that for many it has actually gotten worse with no hope of improvement. Millions of young people are suspended in "limbo." They leave their countries to find better livelihoods in wealthier countries where usually they are only met with disappointment and disillusionment. A friend told me, "My soul is in Kampala but my body is trapped here in Johannesburg." Living conditions have become more difficult especially for immigrants in the wealthy countries as the rich countries have to take care of their own citizens first. This is forcing many immigrants to trek back home in large numbers to face a bleak and uncertain future. The situation in some African countries is so terrible that the immigrants would rather die in the counties they live. One young man, working as a gardener, in Durban, South Africa, told me that it is better for him to be in prison in South Africa than to be a free person in his home country, Malawi.

This reminds me of the anguish of a Zambian taxi driver who asked me, "What is wrong with us as Zambians? Many years ago, they were telling us that we had problems because we did not have many educated people? Now we have many educated people but the problems only seem to be increasing? What is the real cause of the problems?" These questions are a summary of the story of 21st century Africa. In most African countries today, Marcus Garvey's vision of "a new world of black men, not peons, serfs, dogs and slaves, but a nation of sturdy men making their impress upon civilization and causing a new light to dawn upon the human race" (Grant, 2009: 52) is still a far-fetched dream.

CHAPTER 3: A SUMMARY OF *ANIMAL FARM*

Introduction

The stark parallel between the failure of leadership and governance in Africa and the story in *Animal Farm* makes an interesting case and reading. *Animal Farm* is a fictitious story by George Orwell written in 1948. In the story animals on a farm revolt against the owner of the farm with the aim of freeing themselves from the injustices of the owner, Mr. Jones, and of establishing self rule. The idea of revolution is brought about by an elderly pig, Old Major. The essence of the book *Animal Farm* is captured in its blurb,

> Old Major dreamt of a world where all animals are equal and Man is no more. When he tells the other animals on the farm of his vision, his words have a dramatic effect, and the more intelligent animals immediately begin to prepare for the Great Rebellion. The pigs are the cleverest, so naturally it falls on them to teach and organize the others.
>
> Mr. Jones the farmer soon gives up the fight, and the animals rejoice in their victory. But things are not to run so smoothly for long. More humans return to attack them, and the animals find new and unexpected problems surfacing to taint their glorious freedom. As time goes on the pigs lose sight of many of Old Major's maxims, and the new regime feels more and more like the bad old days of Mr. Jones' reign of terror.

Written many years before any African country had become independent (of course minus the odd cases of Liberia and Ethiopia), the story of *Animal Farm* is basically a kind of a prophetic story, an allegory of post-colonial Africa. Most people in many African countries, like the animals in *Animal Farm*, feel that, what Africa has achieved after independence is to have new faces in the state houses but the oppressive system left by the colonialists is still intact. Every new leader seems to come with promises of a better life for the masses but ends up taking the people back to the same situation he or she found them, and sometimes even worse.

In this chapter, we will summarize the story of *Animal Farm* with the aim of establishing a solid understanding of what I call *animal farm systems* prevalent in many (African) countries today. If leadership is to be effective in Africa, leadership change efforts must move beyond changing faces or individuals or replacing them with other individuals to changing or overhauling the systems.

Animal Farm—the story

The vision

The book, *Animal Farm,* begins with a description of Mr. Jones who is depicted as an uncaring and irresponsible person to the animals on the farm. As soon as Mr. Jones goes to sleep, the animals call for an impromptu meeting to hear a strange dream that Old Major, the most respected animal, a pig, on the farm, had had the previous night. The book describes the different animals on the farm and their characters. Some are described as serious minded while the others are just "also runs." Of interest are Mollie, the mare, who is more interested in drawing attention to her red ribbon, than the meeting itself; and the cat who sleeps throughout the whole meeting. Another one is Boxer who has no critique at all.

Then comes the speech, which rather than being about Old Major's dream, turns out to be about the vision he has about the liberation of the animals from servitude to Man in general and Mr. Jones in particular. He eloquently and passionately describes the "current pathetic situation of animal life" (p 3). He stresses that no animal in England knows the meaning of happiness or leisure after he is a year old. No animal in England is free. The life of an animal is one of misery and slavery, he stresses. He then goes on to dismiss the thinking that this is part of the order of nature and squarely places the blame on Man. He emphasizes that "man is the only creature that consumes without producing. He does not give milk, he does not lay eggs, he is too weak to pull the plough and he cannot run fast enough to catch rabbits and yet he is Lord of all animals" (p 4). He pushes on to say if the animals can remove Man from the scene, they will have dealt with the root cause of their hunger and overwork forever.

Old Major hits the climax of his speech, stressing the heart of the message: "This is my message to you comrades: rebellion" (p 5).

With this he incites and fires up the animals to action and an uprising, "Fix your eyes on the rebellion, comrades, throughout the short remainder of your lives" (p 5).

Old major concludes his visionary speech by laying out "the rules of conduct after Man is gone." "Remember," he says, "in fighting Man we must not come to resemble him. After conquering him, do not adopt his vices, therefore: No animal must ever live in a house, or sleep in a bed, or wear clothes, or drink alcohol, or smoke tobacco, or touch money, or engage in trade . . . and above all no animal must ever tyrannize over his own kind. No animal must kill any other animal. All animals are equal" (p 6).

The meeting ends with Old Major teaching the animals a liberation song which throws the animals into a liberation frenzy.

The revolution

Old Major's speech was quickly organized into a system of thought called Animalism. Three pigs, who emerged as natural leaders among the animals, gave themselves the task to teach the other animals the tenets of animalism. At first they met a lot of stupidity and apathy. Some of the remarks from some of the animals included: We have a duty of loyalty to the master; Mr. Jones feeds us, if he were gone we should starve to death. Why should we care about what happens after we are dead? If this rebellion is to happen anyway, what difference does it make whether we work for it or not? Mollie the mare was more worried, she asked, "Will there still be sugar after the rebellion?" and "Shall I be allowed to wear ribbon in my mane?" (pp 9, 10). When the pigs tried to explain to her that her ribbons were a badge of slavery and therefore not necessary, she "agreed" but did not sound convinced.

Another hurdle the pigs had to surmount was the lies of Moses, the tame raven. Moses was a spy for Mr. Jones and a tale bearer. He kept preaching to the other animals that he knew about the existence of a mysterious country called

Sugar Candy Mountain, to which all animals went when they died. He claimed that in Sugar Candy Mountain it is Sunday seven days a week, clover was in season all year round; and lump sugar and linseed cake grew on hedges. The pigs had a very hard time to convince the animals that such a place does not exist and to encourage them to concentrate on improving their own lot here on earth instead of waiting to enjoy after they are dead.

Within a short time, Mr. Jones was overthrown through the rebellion and uprising. He and his people were chased out of the farm. The animals were very excited. The farm was finally theirs. After inspecting Mr. Jones house and all its constituents, they all agreed that the house should not be destroyed but be kept as a museum. The name of the farm was changed from Manor Farm to Animal Farm. Then they wrote down the seven unalterable commandments of animalism that all the animals must adhere to (p 15):

1. Whatever goes up on two legs is an enemy
2. Whatever goes upon four legs, or has wings, is a friend
3. No animal shall wear clothes
4. No animal shall sleep in a bed
5. No animal shall drink alcohol
6. No animal shall harm any other animal
7. All animals are equal

The first task was to milk the cows. After milking the cows, there were five buckets of frothing milk. When some animals asked what was going to happen to the milk, Napoleon, the leader of the pigs and by extension the leader of the animals, told them not to worry about the milk. He assured them the milk would be "taken care of." When they came back from harvesting, the animals noticed that the milk had disappeared. No explanation was given and no one questioned.

A taste of freedom

The animals had a promising start. The harvest was much larger than hoped for. There was so much happiness and so much satisfaction that the food was truly theirs, produced by themselves for themselves, and not doted to them by a grudging master. The animals were so motivated, every animal working according to their capacity except for Boxer the horse who worked more than anybody else. He gave himself as his personal motto: I will work harder.

The animals came up with a flag to symbolize their new found autonomy and held weekly meetings where the work of the coming week was planned out and resolutions were put forward and debated. It was always the pigs who put forward the resolutions. The other animals understood how to vote but could not think of any resolutions of their own. They also formed various committees: egg production committee for the hens, clean tails league for the cows, wild comrades' re-education committee (to tame the rats and rabbits). They also had the whiter wool movement for the sheep and many others. The performance of the committees was generally weak except for the reading and writing classes. The pigs could read and write perfectly. The dogs learnt to read fairly well but were not interested in reading anything except the seven commandments of animalism. A few other animals learnt how to read and write but they generally did not exercise that faculty. None of the other animals went beyond the letter A. Most of the stupider animals could not memorize the seven commandments by heart. To help them, the seven commandments were condensed for them to, "four legs good, and two legs bad" (p 21).

Tell tale signs

Napoleon believed that the education of the young was more important than that of the adults. Soon after two dogs gave birth to nine puppies Napoleon took them away to take personal responsibility for their training. It was later discovered that the milk which had disappeared was actually being mixed everyday into the pigs mash.

The pigs ordered all the apples to be collected to the harness room for use by the pigs. Some of the animals murmured but it was of no use because all the pigs were in agreement. Napoleon's spokesperson, Squealer, was sent to explain to the animals why it was necessary for the pigs to have the apples. He explained,

> Comrades, you do not imagine, I hope, that we pigs are doing this in the spirit of selfishness and privilege? Many of us actually dislike milk and apples. I dislike them myself. Our sole object is taking these things to preserve our health. Milk and apples (this has been proven by science, comrades), contain substances absolutely necessary to the well being of a pig. We pigs are brain workers. The whole management and organization of this farm depends on us. Day and night we are watching over your welfare. It is for your sake that we drink that milk and eat those apples. Do you know what would happen if we pigs failed our duty? Jones would come back—surely there is no one among you who wants Jones to come back? (p 22).

With this line of argument it was agreed that milk and apples should be kept for the pigs alone.

Managing opposition

Mollie defected to another farm. Apparently she participated in removing Mr. Jones from the farm but she did not remove Mr. Jones from her heart. Napoleon and Snowball, another pig, a leader, continually showed dissent to each other's views on every major point. It soon became clear that the farm had two leaders with each having his following of loyalists. This led to bitter politicking between the two.

Snowball was more articulate, visionary and innovative and had constructive plans on how to improve the farm. Napoleon did not have any plans but quietly insinuated that Snowball's plans would come to nothing. After completing the plan for a windmill, all the animals came to excitedly see it, except Napoleon who came last only to urinate on it. He then argued that the urgent need of the farm was to increase food production not the proposed windmill. Putting efforts on the windmill would make the animals starve to death.

Napoleon and Snowball also disagreed on the defense of the farm. Napoleon believed they should buy firearms and train themselves in the use of the firearms. Snowball believed that they needed to send out more and more pigeons to stir up rebellion among the animals in the other farms. The one argued that if they did not defend themselves, they would be conquered while the other argued that if rebellions occurred everywhere, there would be no need to defend themselves. The animals did not know who of the two to believe as each sounded right. They then decided to believe the one who was speaking at the moment. The endless debate and politicking between Napoleon and Snowball ended with Snowball being brutally chased out of the farm by the dogs Napoleon had been "training." The dogs wagged their tails to Napoleon the same way they did to Mr. Jones.

To the surprise of all the animals, Napoleon, mounting on the floor where Old Major made his visionary speech, decreed that from then on the Sunday morning meetings would come to an end. They were unnecessary and a waste of time. From then on all questions relating to the running of the farm would be settled by a special committee of pigs, presided over by him. The committee will give orders and there will be no more debates. Any animal trying to question the decision was quickly intimidated and silenced.

Squealer was sent again to explain to the animals on the new arrangement. He explained that Napoleon will be able to make better decisions than the rest of the animals. On Snowball, he says that in fact, Snowball was an enemy to all the animals on the farm and he encouraged them to be loyal, obedient and disciplined. He finishes by saying that if these are not followed, Mr. Jones may come back. In reaction to this, Boxer, the horse adds to his motto "I will work harder" (p 35) another one "Napoleon is always right" (p 35). He said he adopted this new motto to save himself from the contradiction of what he was seeing in the conduct of Napoleon and the pigs on one hand; and what Squealer was saying on the other.

The sitting arrangements at the meetings also changed. They no longer sat together. Napoleon, Squealer and another pig, Minimus (a composer of praise songs and poems for Napoleon) sat in front with all the other pigs behind them and the dogs forming a semi-circle around the three. Napoleon reads out the orders of the week in a soldierly style and dismisses the meeting without discussion. In one of the meetings, to the surprise of everyone, Napoleon, announces that Snowball's plan for the windmill will be implemented after all. He does not give any reason for the "sudden" change of mind. Squealer goes to work again explaining that Napoleon had not really opposed the Windmill project. In fact the plan that Snowball drew had been stolen from among Napoleon's papers. In fact the idea was Napoleon's creation. With some intimidation from the dogs, the animals accepted the explanation without further question.

Hardships and blame game

Material progress seemed to be slowing down and the animals only consolation was their sense of freedom and independence. Making the windmill seemed to be a tall order. The animals also begin facing challenges in finding what they could not produce on the farm: paraffin oil, nails, string, dog biscuits, and iron for the horses' shoes; seeds, fertilizers; and various tools for the windmill. To address these challenges Napoleon comes up with a new policy stating that from now on Animal Farm would engage in trade with neighboring farms; not of course for any commercial purposes but simply to obtain certain materials which were urgently necessary. The animals are shocked, but they are shocked even more to learn that arrangements had already been made and that Napoleon himself would handle the trade personally. Squealer goes around telling the animals that the resolution against trade and using money was never passed or even suggested. It was pure imagination, probably circulated by Snowball. The animals were hesitantly convinced.

The animals were actually proud to see their leader Napoleon, on all fours, giving orders to the solicitor standing on his two legs. Although the humans hated Animal Farm and looked forward to the day it would fall, they acknowledged the efficiency of the farm and finally began to call it by its proper name, Animal Farm.

Around this time, the pigs suddenly moved into the farmhouse left by Mr. Jones and took up residence there. Squealer explained to the other animals that the pigs had to do this because it was necessary for the pigs to have a quiet place to work from and that the house was more suited to the dignity of a leader. When the animal check on the seven commandments of animalism, they observe that the fourth commandment had been modified to read, "no animal shall sleep in a bed *between sheets*" (p 42).

In an unfortunate event, the windmill which was half built by this time is completely damaged by a whirlwind; this is blamed on the ousted Snowball who later is turned into a myth visiting the farm at night and capable of advising the animals in their dreams to rebel against Napoleon. In effect, Snowball had been turned into an invisible influence pervading the air about the animals and menacing them with all kinds of dangers. Whenever something went wrong, it was blamed on Snowball. Anyone expressing dissent was said to be in league with Snowball.

Tyranny

Conditions continued to worsen on the farm with an imminent starvation. Napoleon hired a propagandist to spread contrary rumors among the surrounding farms. The hens try to protest against a command by Napoleon for them to supply eggs for sale to keep the farm afloat until summer. The hens insist that selling eggs now would be murder. They make determined efforts to thwart Napoleon's wishes. Napoleon acted swiftly and ruthlessly by ordering the hens' ration to be stopped and that any animal giving them any help should be punished by death. The hens try to hold out for five days but eventually capitulate and go back to their nesting boxes. Nine hens die as a result but it was recorded that they died of coccidiosis.

Napoleon continued to accord himself many accolades including animal hero, first class and animal hero second class.

The tyranny reached a new high when four pigs are dragged to the front of the animals at a meeting and asked to confess their crimes. Apparently, under some hypnosis or manipulation the pigs confess that they were in league with Snowball and so did a few chickens, a goose, some sheep and many other animals that were all promptly killed. The animals were shaken and miserable. Boxer's response was rather confusing. He says,

> I do not understand it. I would not have believed that such things could happen on our farm. It must be due to some fault in ourselves. The solution as I see it is to work harder. From now onwards I shall get up a full hour earlier in the mornings (p 54).

Boxer was obviously in denial and refused to see any wrongdoing in the leader Napoleon. All the animals could not understand why and how they had come to a time when no one dared speak his mind, when fierce growling dogs roamed everywhere.

Later, four chickens were executed for allegedly plotting to assassinate Napoleon. Additional security measures were immediately instituted including a young pig to taste all the food before Napoleon ate it lest it should be poisoned.

The animals are hit by another decree from Napoleon that the revolutionary song, "Beasts of England," had since been abolished and replaced with a more domesticating song called "a call to loyalty"—"Animal Farm, Animal Farm, never through me shall you come to harm" (p 56).

Big man politics

The sixth commandment, "no animal shall kill another animal," had been secretly altered to "no animal shall kill another animal *for no cause*" (p 56). The animals were confused but could not properly recall the last words. Meanwhile Napoleon continues to consolidate his power adding a cockerel to his convoy and commanded that the gun must be fired on his birthday. From now on it was wrong to call him just Napoleon. He had to be called Our Leader, Comrade Napoleon together with a string of titles including Father of all Animals, Terror of Mankind, Protector of the Sheepfold, Ducklings' Friends etc. In his speeches Squealer talks about Napoleon with tears flowing down his cheeks about Napoleon's wisdom, the goodness of his heart and the deep love he bore to all animals everywhere especially the unhappy animals that still lived in ignorance and slavery on the other farms.

The animals were made to give credit for every successful achievement and good fortune. "Under the guidance of our leader, Comrade Napoleon, I have laid five eggs in six days," a hen would say, or the cows at a pool would sing, "Thanks to the leadership of Comrade Napoleon, how excellent this water tastes" (p 58). Songs and poems were composed in honor of the name of Napoleon.

After so many hurdles the windmill was completed. Napoleon called it Napoleon mill. Napoleon surprises the animals once more by announcing a done deal with Frederick, a farmer from a nearby farm that the animals believed was their sworn enemy. All relationships with Foxwood had been broken off and insulting messages had been sent to Pilkington, the owner of the farm who had been a long time friend of Animal Farm. Animal farm convinces the animals that all the horrifying stories they used to hear about Frederick were not true or they were grossly exaggerated. Soon after, it turned out that Frederick defrauded Napoleon and the animals. He got the timber for nothing. And soon after this, Frederick attacks Animal Farm with his men, blasting the Napoleon Windmill down in the process. Efforts to get help from Pilkington prove futile.

After a drinking party and a hangover Napoleon buys some books on brewing and distilling and commanded growing of barley. The fifth commandment "no animal shall drink alcohol" was changed to "no animal shall drink alcohol *in excess*" (p 79).

True colors

Jones and all he stood for had almost faded out of memory to the animals since most of them were new and were not there during the time of the rebellion. Life was hard but Squealer kept telling them that it was much better now than it was during the era of Mr. Jones.

Napoleon was the only boar responsible for fathering all the pigs. The pigs were now given extra status. Whenever a pig was passing by, all the other animals were asked to step aside. In addition, the pigs were given the privilege to wear green ribbons on their tails on Sundays. While rations for all the animals were being reduced, the pigs looked much happier and healthier than the others.

Animal farm was declared a republic and Napoleon its obvious President. He was the only candidate and was elected unanimously.

One evening, Boxer, the hardworking horse, fell down due to exhaustion and a bad lung. Squealer rushes to the scene and assures the other animals: "Comrade Napoleon had learnt with the very deepest distress of the misfortunes to one of the most loyal workers on the farm and that he had made arrangements for him to be taken to hospital" (p 78).

The animals learnt later that the so-called hospital was actually a slaughter house for horses, but about it, Squealer manages to convince them otherwise. He encourages the animals to adopt Boxer's two mottos, "I will work hard." and "Napoleon is always right." as a befitting memory for a good friend. The money from Boxer's slaughter is used to buy whisky for the pigs.

Full circle

The book finishes with a climax, albeit a negative one. It is an apogee of disillusionment among the animals—a kind of full circle, back to the point the situation was at the beginning of the book.

Years had passed and different generations of animals had come and gone. No one remembered the old days before the rebellion. To many of the young animals, the rebellion was just a dim tradition. Many of the new animals were very stupid and could not learn the alphabet beyond the letter B and believed everything they were told without questioning.

The farm itself had actually grown richer but without making the animals themselves any richer except the pigs and the dogs whose work was "supervision and management" which they claimed the other animals were too ignorant to understand. The idea of setting aside a part of the farm for retired animals had since been dropped and no animal ever retired.

Most of the animals did not know their lives had really improved since the rebellion or not. Only Benjamin who had been suspicious all along could say with certainty that nothing had changed and to him hunger, hardship and disappointment were the unalterable law of life. Talk on the farm was less on the future but on the good old days and achievements of the past.

One evening the animals were shocked to see Squealer and all the pigs including Napoleon himself, walking on their two legs. This was the final unmasking of the pigs. The song "four legs good, two legs bad" was changed to "four legs good, two legs better." The seven commandments were finally replaced, unilaterally by Napoleon, with a single commandment, "all animals are equal *but some animals are more equal than others*" (p 84).

The pigs were now supervising the other animals on two feet with whips in their hands and they were now wearing Mr. Jones' clothes. They had subscribed to newspapers and were planning to install a telephone. The farm began receiving human visitors who met the pigs on terms of equality.

In a meeting that the animals eavesdrop and are watching from the windows, Mr. Pilkington, leader of the human delegation is giving a speech. He said he was happy because a long period of misunderstanding and mistrust had now come to an end. He ended his speech by emphasizing that there was no need for any continued clashes of interest between pigs and human beings because their struggles and difficulties were one. Napoleon and the pigs had the lower animals to contend with while he and his people had the lower class to contend with. He congratulated the pigs on giving the lower animals low rations, long working hours and a general absence of pampering.

In his reply Napoleon dismissed the rumor that he and the animals were planning to spread rebellion to the surrounding farms. He said Animal Farm was a cooperative enterprise and that the title deeds were owned jointly by the pigs. He then abolished all rituals on the farm like calling each other comrade, saluting the flag and Sunday meetings. To crown it all, the Name Animal Farm would revert to its old and 'proper' farm, Manor Farm. He finishes his speech to a toast for Manor Farm.

The meeting reaches a climax, as the pigs in the eyes of the animals could no longer be differentiated in appearance from the human beings. As the pigs and human beings were quarrelling over a game of cards, it was no longer possible to say which was human and which was pig.

Conclusion

Animal farm starts with high hopes and promise of freedom for all animals but this feeling was to be short-lived. The animals had managed to remove Mr. Jones but they did not remove Mr. Jones' system. Old Major's vision was hijacked by a small elite, who, soon after taking power, began to unmask themselves until finally, "Mr. Jones" had returned in the form of Napoleon and his cronies. The original "constitution" was gradually altered until all the laws of animalism were changed and replaced with Mr. Jones' old laws of oppression.

All opposition was brutally crushed. All failures by the leadership were blamed on "dissidents" working from outside the farm. The leader continued to confer upon himself one accolade after another and his opulence and that of his cronies knew no bounds while the poverty of the rest of the animals was becoming more and more unbearable. The climax is when Napoleon openly declares that the name of the farm, Animal Farm, had reverted to its original and proper name, Manor Farm.

The only prediction one can make after reading the animal farm story is that the farm was ripe for another revolution, this time from the young and new animals who knew nothing about the first revolution. But whether they would be able to break the system, and not just remove Napoleon and his cronies, is another question. *Animal Farm* was a perfect prophetic parable for Africa and its leadership and governance.

Soon after independence from the colonial masters, there was a lot of momentum, excitement and hope for the new era of independence in Africa. Today, more than half a century later, the hope is less alive. While there is more and more talk about the "rise of Africa," most ordinary citizens cannot say with certainty whether they are any better off than their parents were before independence. In many instances they are actually poorer. Like Benjamin in *Animal Farm*, the lived experience of many on the continent is that "nothing has changed; hunger; hardship and disappointment are the unalterable law of life."

Constitutions are altered beyond recognition in favor of ruling presidents and MPs. Presidents and their cronies live in unbelievable opulence while the masses continue to sink into an abyss of poverty. The masses are always confused when they hear the leaders say their countries are developing as they have no evidence in their personal lives of the claimed development. Huge amounts of money are still spent on propaganda with the aim of domesticating the minds of unsuspecting illiterate masses in order to suppress critique. Dissent and expression of different opinions are still a crime and punishable by a diverse means in many a place.

Like Napoleon in the *Animal Farm* story, many African leaders exhibit the colonial masters' behaviors exponentially. In the words of Chika Onyeani (2000: 99,100):

> The African leader inherited the European's position; he inherited his huge offices; he inherited his more than 10 messengers; he inherited his sex on demand from his numerous secretaries; he inherited his disrespect for his subordinates; he inherited more than three cars; he inherited his huge house with several servants and drivers. He inherited his demand for unquestioned authority and obedience. He was pampered beyond human endurance by the masses who expected to see a difference from the colonial behavior. Instead, they found that the behavior in most cases was more tyrannical than his colonial predecessor.

Each succeeding leader seems to build on the tyranny of his or her predecessor. This is because they are products of the same system. Real development will not happen until animal farm systems are broken. Removing Mr. Jones did not change the system. Similarly removing one leader and replacing him or her with another does not necessarily change the system.

CHAPTER 4: SYSTEMS IN PRACTICE

Introduction

In this chapter, I present five cases to illustrate the systems within which the individual presidents are operating. In all the cases, the individuals inherited a system that they did not consciously undertake to destroy and replace with new and genuinely more empowering and democratic ones. It can also be argued that by consciously or unconsciously perpetuating the systems they found, they entrenched the key animal farm system characteristic of "it's-our-time-to-feast attitude" for the future leaders. In other words, they will hand over the same system to the leaders who will succeed them. This leaves the future or destiny of a country at the mercy of the character of the leaders who will succeed the individuals (that is, if they will be powerful enough to recognize and destroy the animal farm systems). A proper system on the other hand puts the future and destiny of the country in the hands of all the citizens, not in the hands of fate. A good system is the only way to prevent countries and indeed the entire continent from going in cycles.

1. Senegal—Abdoulaye Wade, Senegal

Brief history

Abdoulaye Wade was born in 1926 though some people claim that he was born much earlier since around that time record keeping was very poor and unreliable. He was the first dean of the College of Law and Economic Sciences at the University of Dakar. Abdoulaye Wade holds two doctorate degrees in law and in economics. He also received an honorary doctor of Law degree from the University of Minnesota. Abdoulaye Wade played a key role in the formation and launching of the New Partnership for Africa's Development (NEPAD). He was the President of Senegal and Secretary General of the Senegalese Democratic Party. He led the party since it was established in 1974. He was a long-time opposition leader and ran for presidency four times beginning 1978.

Presidency

Abdoulaye Wade became President in 2000. He was elected for a second term of office in 2007 in a controversial election in which the main opposition parties did not accept his victory and disputed his legitimacy as President. Wade responded by saying there would no longer be possibility for dialogue with opposition unless they recognized him as a legitimate President.

Senegal had a constitutional seven year term for the Presidency which in 2007 was reduced to five. In 2008, the term limit was reverted to the original seven years through constitutional change by the National Assembly. Although this change would not apply to the incumbent President, Wade, he declared that he would run for a Third Term in 2012. He confirmed this decision in 2009. Officially, Wade had no plans to leave office as long as his health was in good condition. In case his health failed, he was grooming his son, Karim, to succeed him. The people were generally angry with Mr. Wade's decision to stand again for Presidency in 2012 for a Third Term in Office when he would be 86. In June, 2011, he introduced a bill in parliament to reduce the winning percentage of presidents' votes from 50 percent plus one person to 25 percent. This triggered high tension and widespread riots especially by the youth. With increasing pressure, he was forced to withdraw the proposal from parliament. A few days later, the youths got bolder and staged more protests and clashed with the police in Dakar, asking the President to step down because of increased frequency of electricity blackouts in the country which would at times last four days. The youths attacked and burnt government buildings, blocked and burnt vehicles.

Accusations

Wade was accused of corruption, nepotism and constraints on freedoms of the press and civil liberties. He was also accused by Christian Bishops for publicly denying the divinity of Christ and comparing Christ to the statue in the African Renaissance Monument. He later regretted that his comments had caused offence to Christians.

President Wade was accused of excessive spending, including the commissioning of the 160-foot bronze statue, also known as the African Renaissance Monument for which Wade claimed he was entitled to 35 percent of all tourist profits it generates because of the intellectual property for conceiving the idea. In 2009, Wade was criticized for a "good bye present" he reportedly gave to a departing IMF official. It was a big bag of money worthy $200,000.00.

In 2010 Mr. Wade bought one of French President Nicholas Sarkozy's planes at the price of 32 million Euros. *Mail and Guardian* of November 12, 2010 quoted an opposition leader, Helen Tine, saying, "I am shocked. We cannot understand that in the difficult economic context faced by the Senegalese, we can allow this expense which is neither relevant nor a priority." She further said it was a crime against the people of Senegal. She went as far as saying, "People who make such decisions are mentally unbalanced."

This purchase was against a background of rising food prices, high unemployment especially among the youths, and daily power outages which angered and frustrated many people including many former supporters of the President. They were also angered by his decision to hand over several important government posts to his son Karim. The general feeling among the population was one of disillusionment as there was a lot of hope and trust when Wade came into power in 2000. People felt they had been totally deceived.

Popular reactions

A protest march was organized in Dakar on 19th March 2011 to protest against general unhappiness with the regime and rising cost of living. Reporting on the march, VOA observed, "The turnout was impressive, by some estimates as many as 3,000 attended, though at times there appeared to be more onlookers than participants." Wade responded to the march with a national televised speech recorded by VOA. Part of the speech is reproduced below:

> I have been to Mali, Gambia and Morocco. Most of our African countries have compared standards of living; it is tough but the populations manage in

however ways they can to sustain a living and possibly lift themselves out of poverty. I am saying this to point out that regimes are not 100 percent responsible for the state of our countries: we are poor nations, that are just the bottom line so we should not expect the living standards of rich countries.

One example: in Senegal people complain about frequent electricity outages but the electricity company has old equipment while urban population consumption continues to climb at an alarming rate. It is obvious that the electricity company will struggle to provide sustained energy under these circumstances, the situation might improve but it will take time. It will require innovation to implement a successful solution.

But the government should not be blamed for this . . . and our opponents should not cause chaos in an already poor country.

Author observation

It is important to note that the assertion that Africa is poor has often been used by leaders to entrench a poverty mentality in their people rather than motivate them to be outraged about *the status quo* and do something about it. The leaders have also used the poverty tagline to sell Africa to the rest of the world. Today, Africa is primarily associated with poverty. When most people hear the word, Africa, the first thought that comes to their mind is poverty. It is true that Africa is poor but leaders would do better to emphasize to the people that poverty is not a divine decree; it is not normal and should not be permanent. They should work with and encourage the people to fight rather than accept poverty.

On Saturday, 28th January, 2012 violence erupted in Dakar after a constitutional court ruled that Abdoulaye Wade could stand for a third term in office. He won the first round of the elections with 34 percent while his major opponent got 26 percent. After a second round he lost the elections.

2. Malawi—Bingu wa Mutharika

Born Brightson Webster Ryson Thom, Bingu wa Mutharika was born on February 24, 1934. He was among the 32 beneficiaries of Malawi's first President Hastings Kamuzu Banda's initiative to "fast-track diplomas to replace the white dominated civil service" soon after independence. The group traveled to India on an Indira Gandhi Scholarship Scheme where he managed to stay on and eventually obtained bachelors and masters degrees. He eventually got a doctorate in development economics from Pacific Western University.

Presidency

Mutharika became Malawi's third President on 24th May, 2004 after winning a disputed election. He won with 31 percent of the votes. He won on the ticket of the United Democratic Front (UDF), the party of the former President, Bakili Muluzi. His first term in office was highly praised both at home and abroad. He managed to stabilize a wrecked economy and his greatest achievement was to ensure food security for the nation which earned him international recognition and admiration. He managed to restore international goodwill which had largely been destroyed by the previous Bakili Muluzi regime. He was also strong at fighting corruption which culminated in charging the former President on alleged theft of public funds in office amounting to about $100 million. Against a background of Malawi's poor infrastructure, several construction projects were in progress and there were high levels of excitement and enthusiasm throughout the country. A lot of young people who had fled the country during Mr. Muluzi's regime returned to the "new opportunities" back home.

In February, 2005, I traveled to Washington DC, USA to launch my first book, *Understanding Organizational Sustainability through African Proverbs.* On the plane from Lilongwe, Malawi to Johannesburg, South Africa, the President and his wife joined us as he was traveling to Taiwan. There was perceptible excitement in the plane as the President came from his first class section to "interact" with the people in the economy class. Excited parents handed over their babies to him and asked for photos. He walked in the aisles and talked to people.

I took the opportunity to meet him. I asked for permission from the chief body guard who went to consult with him. He came back and signaled me to go in. I had a brief meeting with him for 10 minutes. I handed him a copy of my book. He said, "I'm pleased with the work young people like you are doing in putting Malawi on the world map through creativity."

He encouraged me to go to the Malawian embassy when I arrived in the US and that they should give me all the support I needed while in the US. He also encouraged me to make an effort to see him when I was back. I excitedly went out and back to my seat in the economy class.

After many months I was happy to hear him use one of the folktales in the book I gave him. It told me he had read the book as he had promised.

Many people appreciated his decision to build a $620,000 mausoleum for the late President Hastings Kamuzu Banda in order to "put history in perspective."

Bingu wa Mutharika was perceived by many to be introducing a new type of progressive leadership in the country. He had a strong and forward looking vision: to turn Malawi from being a predominantly importing nation to a predominantly middle income exporting country; he also came up with a well articulated strategy to turn the vision to reality: to establish an agricultural green built along the shores of Lake Malawi and the Shire River. Lake Malawi covers one third of Malawi's surface areas. The Green Built initiative would ensure permanent food security for the country and would turn Malawi into the bread basket for Southern Africa and beyond. Malawi being a landlocked country, he would surmount this challenge by building an inland port on the Shire River that would connect Malawi to the Indian Ocean through the Zambezi River. Added to this he planned to build five universities to ensure that the country reaches an intellectual threshold that would back and drive these and other initiatives and opportunities. Coupled to all these Bungu wa Mutharika had among his advisors some of the best brains, in their fields, in the world. What else does one need to be a good leader and to make impact?

Second term

Against this background, Malawians voted massively for Mutharika giving him a second term mandate in 2009. He won with a landslide. Expectations were high for another five years of progress and development. But the people should have known better.

Just before the elections, the President announced that he was the patron of his tribal group—Mulhakho wa Alhomwe—which was formed to preserve the culture and promote the interests of the Alhomwe people—a minority tribe in the country. A number of people questioned the wisdom of a head of state being patron of one particular tribe in a country with several tribes. Civil society and religious leaders raised concern that there was a feeling that members of the tribal group were being favored in allocation of opportunities in the country. They felt the President was symbolically moving away from a national to a tribal podium.

The President then announced that "to reflect the development progress the country had achieved in his five-year rule" he was going to change or modify the national flag. There were loud protests from many quarters but he went ahead and changed the flag "after wide consultations with the people," he claimed.

In 2010, less than one year after winning his second term bid, the President's party began campaigning for Mutharika's brother as a the presidential candidate for the next 2014 elections. This move caused some hiccups in the party. Cabinet ministers and members of parliament were expected to endorse the president's brother to show loyalty. Those that did not were fired or reprised. One person to be shown the exit door for not towing the line was the Vice President, Joyce Banda. When asked why he had fired the Vice President, according to *The Daily Times* of Monday 9 May, 2011, the President explained his action,

> When God noted that Lucifer was being big headed, he did not hesitate to evict him from heaven. So, before you start faulting me for being intolerant because I have sacked Joyce Banda from DPP, fault God for sacking Lucifer from heaven.

In 2009, the President bought a Presidential private jet costing $22 million. Official reports declared that it was bought at a much lower price. The maintenance and insurance charges on the plane would cost Malawians $300,000 per year. The money was taken from tax payers' money. Mutharika justified the purchase of the jet, stating that the jet has, on the contrary, helped save hard currency as hiring used to cost the economy $10,000/hour. In reaction to this, a comment in *The Weekend Nation* of Saturday, May 28, 2011 read,

> There is nothing more worrying about governance of a country than a government that is economical with the truth. When government bought the Presidential jet in 2009, Malawians were told its cost was $13 million and that it was a cheaper option than chartering planes for the Head of State. But as it has now transpired, thanks to the Department for International Development, the plane did not only cost $22 million, our research has also shown that the jet is draining public coffers of the already scarce resources. In a country that has conflicting needs in sectors such as health and education, one expects

> government to be transparent, accountable and prudent when purchasing expensive property, such as the jet, whose cost is shouldered by tax payers.
>
> While we do not expect the President to travel like a commoner when discharging public duties, we expect those in government to make practical decisions that make economic sense without overburdening the taxpayer. Was the purchase of the jet really necessary? Was an open and thorough cost benefit analysis conducted before the jet was bought? Why did government hide the real cost of the jet from tax payers? Can our poor economy sustain the running of this jet? Perhaps our leaders should learn to be truthful with the country's citizens who put them in the positions they are holding. The people deserve nothing but the truth, especially when it comes to how government is spending their hard earned tax.

The purchase of the plane was followed by nation-wide fuel shortages that never abated. Malawi being a land locked country and getting most of its fuel through Mozambique, the fuel shortages were officially blamed on logistical problems in neighboring Mozambique. The fuel shortages were also officially blamed on externalization of hard currency by the "Malawian Indian traders." After two years of fuel shortages, and after running out of explanations, the Minister of Energy and Mining, Mr. Grain Malunga, was heard on radio advising Malawians, "You should get used to the fuel shortages because the problem would not go away soon." He later claimed that he was misquoted and for sure the fuel scarcity continued unabated. On 11th July, 2011, speaking on Malawi Institute of Journalism (MIJ) Radio, the Presidential Advisor, Dr. Hetherwick Ntaba, told Malawians, "There was nothing unusual with the problems the country was facing because there is no country in the whole world, including the US that does not have problems."

On December 10, 2010, the President suspended the Malawi Electoral Commission for "not being able to account for about $100 million." It was later revealed that it was not true that such an amount of money had gone missing. This raised suspicions that the suspension of the Commission was just a ploy to avoid the then forthcoming local elections which were planned for April 2011. To prove this suspicion, the President announced in May 2011 that the elections had been postponed to 2014, the year of the presidential and parliamentary elections. No explanation was given for the postponement. A large majority of people felt that this was a move to avoid a major embarrassment from the losses the party would incur due to its falling popularity among the people.

In February, 2011, a University of Malawi political science lecturer, Dr. Blessings Chinsinga, gave an example in class, saying the causes of the revolution in the Arab world that time were similar to the situation in the country. For this comment, he was summoned by the Inspector General of police. When he came back and explained to his fellow lecturers, they were angered as they took this to be an infringement on academic freedom. They demanded an apology from the Inspector General of police. The President, who was the official head of police and university at the same time, answered on behalf of the Inspector General, stating that the Inspector General could not apologize because it would be like it was "him (the president) who was apologizing."

"Have you ever seen a President apologizing to a professor anywhere in the world?" he asked a cheering crowd at a public rally.

The University was eventually closed indefinitely by decree from the President. The lecturers went on an indefinite strike and vowed that they would only come back to class if their academic freedom was guaranteed. The stand-off lasted eight months. Amidst growing pressure, the President eventually relented and assured the lecturers of their academic freedom.

At a public rally on 6th March, 2011 Mutharika declared that any group planning to hold a demonstration anywhere in the country should pay a deposit of about $15,000 as surety against any possible damages that may ensue. He also called upon the youths in his party to "protect him" by "dealing with his opponents the same way the young democrats of Bakili Muluzi and Youth Leaguers of Kamuzu Banda did." The Youth Leaguers and the Young Democrats were notorious for physically attacking and persecuting opponents of Kamuzu Banda and Bakili Muluzi respectively. He later clarified at another rally that he did not mean that the young democrats should beat up people but that "when the people do not understand government policy, the young democrats should guide them."

A day before the 20th July mass demonstrations, DPP (party) vehicles paraded Blantyre city centre full of youths brandishing panga knives and threatening to deal with those who would take part in the demonstrations the next day. Soon after the demonstrations, a number of leading civil society leaders were beaten up and threatened by "unknown people." An office and house were torched also by "unknown people." Promises about investigations by government were made but no one was arrested. A student, "who was politically active" much to the distaste of government was murdered at a University campus. Police explained his death as suicide which was dismissed by the pathologist. Again, this act was committed by "unknown people" who were later (after the demise of the President and under a new regime) identified as Bingu wa Mutharika's functionaries.

A leaked document written by the British High Commissioner to his home office raised some of the above issues and it described Mutharika as becoming increasingly "combative" and "autocratic." This irked the President. In a move that surprised most people, the President deported the High Commissioner. Britain was the major donor to Malawi, funding up to a third of the budget annually. Britain reciprocated by deporting the Malawian envoy from London. Relationships soured and Britain withheld its funding to Malawi. This aid withdrawal was similarly taken by other countries such as Norway and Germany who had their own governance concerns over Mutharika's regime.

Officially, the aid withdrawal was blamed on "donors forcing Malawi to allow women to marry fellow women and men to marry fellow men which the President and the government of Malawi were totally against." An opposition MP questioned this notion in parliament by pointing out what he considered to be the real issues. He asked,

> I am worried when I hear government officials telling the nation that donors are pulling out because of gay rights. Oh, no! That is a blatant lie. Is lack of academic freedom a gay right? Is suppression of press and media freedom a gay

> right? Is banning of public demonstrations a gay right? Is nepotism and tribalism a gay right? Is victimization of the Vice President a gay right? Is financial mismanagement a gay right? Is threatening and beating of human rights activists a gay right? (*The Nation*, Wednesday, 25 May, 2011)

Mutharika opened the country's annual tobacco market (tobacco is the major forex earner accounting up to 40% of the county's GDP) of 2011, by castigating the tobacco buyers who are mostly British, calling them thieves, crooks and neo-colonialists. The tobacco prices fell to an all-time low.

With drying donor inflows and not much income from the tobacco sales, the country was, in effect, in an economic crisis. In a move that was not so surprising, the President announced in his state of the nation address at the opening of the parliamentary budgeting session, that the country would adopt a "zero-deficit budget." A zero deficit budget in a layman's language means the country would finance the budget from its own finances without contribution from donors.

A zero deficit budget is obviously a developmental and ideal idea. The challenge observed by commentators in this case was that this was rather a desperate and not a conscious measure. One person had observed of the arrangement, "This is absolutely shocking, a near bankrupt government wants to implement a zero-deficit budget?" He felt they were running away from real issues. "They should be humble. They should identify, surface and confront their contradictions. They are choosing to die instead. The real issue here is to mend relationships with donors rather than experimenting with people's lives."

The Malawi Confederation of Chambers of Commerce and Industry (MCCCI) in *The Nation*, Wednesday, 25 May, 2011, commented that a zero deficit budget would lead to "resources cannibalism," that is to say, domestic resources that were meant for development would now be directed towards financing recurrent expenditure. This would put a halt in building the competitiveness of the economy on which Malawi's future success depends and that Malawi would become an unattractive place for investment and business development. They further emphasized that taking away resources from development to expenditure is tantamount to "delegating our responsibility to destiny's fate." Likely implications for the citizens include increased taxation on an already narrow tax base. The press had already picked that the Malawi Police Service had been ordered to raise adequate revenue to finance own salaries from traffic offences. A zero-deficit budget would also increase pressure on domestic borrowing and the old fashioned currency printing would also be a likely negative measure that government could use to finance the budget.

In the zero-deficit budget, the gap between the monetary allocation to the President and the fired Vice President jumped to a ratio of about 16: 1 with the President getting an annual allocation of $15.6 million and the Vice President getting $0.9 million. A *Malawi News* reporter (June 11–17, 2011) commented that the difference between the President's and the Vice Presidents budget was like day and night.

Mutharika's budget speech in parliament was dubbed, "a promise delivered." It mostly centered on what was achieved the previous year (and not always against what was planned) and then the plans for the next year. He concluded that the "Malawi economic miracle" was on track. Immediately, many commentators described the speech as empty, irrelevant and coming from a leader stuck in the past and oblivious to current realities (*Daily Nation*, 24 May, 2011). In the speech, Mutharika announced that his government was in dialogue with the British government to resolve the differences around the deportation of the high commissioner, a claim the British High Commission office denied the next day.

When asked for their comments on the speech, the EU and American officials present at Parliament when the speech was delivered, were diplomatic in their responses, and said they "found it interesting." It was only the Zimbabwean High Commissioner who said she had found it "progressive." The speech conspicuously avoided what the majority of the people had expected it to cover, pertinent issues of concern to the country: the energy crisis and recurrent fuel shortages, the continued reliance on tobacco which can no longer sustain the economy, the sluggish economy and high cost of living. People also expected the President to talk on his decision to expel the British High Commissioner, the closure of the Universities, delays in civil servants salaries and donors withholding aid. The people expected the President to give an honest explanation of the causes and proposed solutions to these issues.

The President concluded his speech, saying:

> I wish to state that the past year has been a very successful period for our country. In the year 2010, our country has continued to register unprecedented socio-economic growth. The positive achievements speak for themselves. The fruits of our country's development can be clearly seen and validated by every true Malawian who has the interest of this nation at heart. Ours is a promise delivered.

Soon after, a columnist responded,

> Which promise has he kept? Which Malawi is he talking about? The country I know is plagued with persistent fuel and forex shortages, pushing the cost of living every day. It is a country where a big number of public sector workers are going without salaries for up to three months—where public hospitals have no drugs, where hunger and dehumanizing poverty are constant companions for many citizens. The Malawi I know is more divided than it was ten short years ago, characterized by schisms between the ruling party and civil society, the academic community, workers, pensioners, the donor community and ordinary Malawians. The picture I see every day is not a rosy one but a bleak and depressing landscape. That is why I have great difficulties accepting the theme of Mutharika's address—A Promise Delivered.

Of those government MPs who praised Mutharika to the sky because of the speech and his "wise and dynamic leadership," he said, "Either these people are taking Malawians for granted or have completely lost touch with reality." He added, "I did not see leadership on that day. I did not see patriotism. All I saw was sycophancy of the worst kind, blind loyalty and hero worship by legislators we elected to represent us and to make our voices heard; and most importantly, a denial by leaders to accept that there are problems and that they have failed" (*Weekend Nation*, Saturday, May 28, 2011).

What was more disturbing was that among the MPs, were Professors, Doctors, Lawyers, Preachers, and professionals of all types. Do these people honestly need to be reminded that clapping hands for wrong things is a sin?

Three days after the state of the nation address, the President was presiding over a graduation ceremony at one of the Universities that had not been opened since the students closed in December 2010. No official reason was given for the continued closure. In his opening prayer, that took six minutes, the chaplain asked for divine intervention on the issues avoided by the President in his state of the nation address, mentioning the issues one by one and imploring the Lord to intervene and "open the eyes of leadership" to see the gravity of these matters. In a gaffe dubbed, "Bingu wa Mutharika answers prayer" the President told the gathering that he wanted to respond to the prayer and reassured the people that his government was in talks with the British government and reiterated that he had enough justifications to deport the British High Commissioner. Clergy men faulted Mutharika noting that he erred by responding to a prayer which was directed to God and not him and that he was not God to respond to prayer.

A columnist, Ephraim Munthali (*Weekend Nation*, Saturday, May 28, 2011), stated that Mutharika and his administration had taken Malawi on a suicide mission and called on Malawians to "put the DPP-led government on suicide watch." He said,

> For over a year now, all signs have been pointing to an administration on a suicide mission. The pattern of recent government actions has been disturbing. First, the government started fighting almost every section of society—religious leaders, the media, civil society, academics and the judiciary—name them. Later the administration talked of 'drunk, stupid and foolish' Malawians. The offending verbiage was later focused on donors. One of the 'stupid donors' representatives was even booted out of the country . . . after a long journey of lies, deceit, victimization, arrests, witch-hunting, public theft that led to the Electoral Commission's closure and then reopening it, government having run out of time buying mafia-like tactics, has cancelled (not postponed as they claim) the local polls.

When people complained that the President does not listen to advice, Bingu wa Mutharika regularly said that he was a listening president. His spokesperson on the other hand constantly reminded Malawians that the President had a right to listen to advice or not.

On 20th July 2011, massive demonstrations erupted across the country. Citizens were protesting against high cost of living and bad governance. Tens of thousands of people came on the streets. In response to the peaceful demonstrations, the police shot dead twenty one unarmed protestors and injured many more. At an end of year party, the police national research officer confessed that as police they were sorry for the loss of life and that they had "shot the people to death by accident."

Bingu wa Mutharika had a number of titles added to his name. Among the titles were "Latter-day Moses" (from Moses, the liberator of Jews from the tyranny of Pharaoh in biblical times), *Chitsulo cha njanje* (Iron man), "conqueror of hunger," "fountain of development"; and most importantly, *Ngwazi* (former dictator Kamuzu Banda's exclusive title, meaning the number one hero). He was properly addressed as His Excellency the President Ngwazi Professor Bingu wa Mutharika.

By December, 2011, two and a half years before the next presidential elections, many observers were commenting that Malawi had become a failed state characterized by sharp economic decline, criminalization of the state, endemic corruption, authoritarian rule and delegitimization of the state (*The Weekend Nation*, 17–18 December, 2011).

In his Christmas national address, the President urged Malawians to be patriotic, peaceful, forgiving and united. He blamed Satan as the mastermind behind the problems the country was facing. He told Malawians that God never stopped loving them in 2011 and that the devil had failed because that year, "the devil sat on our back."

"The devil brought problems, jealousy, lies and envy that we have never experienced in this country and the whole world but God told him, 'This is not your time,' so the devil has failed, God has triumphed," he told the "God-fearing" nation. He told Malawians, "Our prayer should be: 'God the Creator, when you bless other countries do not pass by Malawi. When you bless other nations in the whole world do not pass by Malawi.'"

In March 2012 the Public Affairs Committee (PAC) a high ranking inter religious civil society organization comprising all the major faiths in the country convened a high level conference in Blantyre. The conference ended with two ultimatums: Bingu wa Mutharika to resign within 60 days or to call for a referendum within 90 days to seek a fresh mandate to continue as President. Bingu defiantly refused both ultimatums. Before the 60 days elapsed, on 5th April, 2012 Bingu collapsed in the State House and was pronounced dead upon arrival at Kamuzu Central Hospital in Lilongwe.

3. Ivory Coast—Laurent Gbagbo

A brief background

Laurent Gbagbo was born on 31st May, 1945. He served as the fourth President of Ivory Coast from 2000 until April, 2011. Gbagbo is a classically educated academic. He is a history Professor by profession. He holds a doctorate degree in history. By 1980, Gbagbo was the director of the Institute of History, Development and African Archaeology at the University of Abdjan. After 20 years in opposition, he became President in 2000. Gbagbo became President after Robert Guei, head of the military junta, barred other leading politicians, including Alassane Outarra, from running for Presidency in the October 2000 Presidential elections. When Guei attempted to rig the elections, Gbagbo claimed victory and his supporters took to the streets toppling Guie.

Ivory Coast became independent from France in 1960. The first President was Felix Houphouet-Boigny. He ruled until 1993. His leadership witnessed remarkable growth especially in the first 20 years when the average growth rate averaged more than seven percent per annum. The economy was based on coffee and cocoa. Ivory Coast is the world's largest producer and exporter of cocoa.

During his time, Houphouet Boigny managed to maintain a stable political and civil profile by his policies of inclusion of all ethnic groups in all public and civil affairs. The coffee and cocoa industries however depended on immigrant labour which was first brought into the country by the French colonialists which President Boigny encouraged to stay on after independence. To respond to the growing demand for labour in the coffee and cocoa industry he initiated policies that encouraged migration from the neighbouring countries. There were also liberal ownership laws to the migrants which resulted in a large number of the migrants settling in the country. By 1998, the immigrants and their descendants accounted for 25 percent of the population. They numbered four million (Ogwang, 2011: 3).

A key challenge that Houphouet Boigny had to deal with was the large inequalities between the North and South as most of the cocoa and coffee plantations, and other natural resources were based in the South. His efforts were not fully successful.

In 1980, coffee and cocoa prices fell on the world market. Living standards in Ivory Coast fell and prices of commodities went through the roof. This resulted in riots and unrest. In an attempt to address the situation, the government removed the taxes for the immigrants working on the cocoa and coffee estates and replaced them with subsidies a move which angered most indigenous Ivorians. As jobs became scarce young people sought employment in the informal sector, which they found out had already been filled by the immigrants. This created strong xenophobia against the immigrants.

According to Langer (2010), the resulting economic difficulties aggravated differences between indigenous Ivorians and immigrants on one hand, and between northerners and locals in the prosperous south on the other. The situation began to be described as "north versus south conflict" because a large number of indigenous Ivorians are from the north while immigrants had settled in the south. Ethnicity therefore became a major political factor in elections in Ivory Coast.

Houphouet's party won the first multi-party democracy in 1990. He died shortly after in 1993. Second multi-party elections were scheduled for 1995. Henri Konan Bedie, Houphouet Boigny's successor blocked Alassane Outtara from standing because his newly formed party, Rally for Republicans posed a serious threat to the Democratic Party of Ivory Coast. Bedie had passed a law barring anyone whose parents were not born in Ivory Coast from running for the presidency. This was the basis for barring Outarra as one of his parents was born in Burkina Faso. Gbagbo, as one of the opposition leaders refused to participate because of the unfair electoral policies. Together with Outarra, they formed an alliance to boycott the elections.

When Bedie won, in an election, perceived by many to be unfair, he proceeded to remove many northerners from government positions. Economic stagnation in Bedie's government led to a coup by Robert Guie in 1999.

Presidency
After his election in 2000, Mr Gbagbo promised to break "personality cult" politics, making it clear that he would not make it mandatory to have his portrait hanging in every office and other public places. He also promised that the national media would no longer be obliged to mention the President in all news programs. But once in office, he went back on most of these promises. News broadcasts highlighted Gbagbo's daily activities. Gbagbo had a reputation of being short-tempered especially against "arrogant" journalists.

Gbagbo was mostly supported by largely the Christian South. His opponents were mostly concentrated in the Muslim North. He took a hard stance against northerners by removing them and excluding them from his government. As a result, some disgruntled groups in the army, mostly from the north attempted an unsuccessful coup in 2001.

On 19th September, 2002 a revolt by the northerners against Gbagbo's government partly failed. The rebels, the New Forces, said their grievance was that their candidate Alassane Outarra had been disallowed from running in the 2000 Presidential elections having been accused by Gbagbo of not being a true Ivorian. This would later become Gbagbo's trend towards inciting ethnic division to maintain power following on the concept of Ivorite.

By the end of September 2002, Ivory Coast was in a full fledged civil war, with the northern part of the country under the control of rebels, the New Forces, who were advancing towards Abdjan, the country's commercial city. Gbagbo sought support from the French who sent troops to reinforce government forces. The French managed to force the rebels to withdraw. In 2004, Gbagbo refused to hold Presidential elections and ordered air strikes against the rebels. In the midst of the air strikes nine French soldiers were killed. The French responded by destroying most of the Ivorian military aircraft. In a counter attack, Gbagbo supporters violently attacked French Ivorians and French nationals.

Towards a crisis
Gbagbo's original mandate as President expired on 30th October 2005. He did not leave office. He amassed support from other African leaders in the African Union to support his bid to refuse to hold elections as promised. On First November, 2006, the UN Security Council endorsed another one year extension to elections.

On 4th March 2007, a peace deal between the rebels, New Forces, and government was signed in Burkina Faso with Guillaume Soro leader of the New Forces becoming the Prime Minister. The elections were further postponed to 2010. In 2009, Gbagbo accused the electoral commission of bloating up the voter registration list with names of people who were not Ivorians. He then dissolved the electoral commission in February 2010 which forced the opposition parties to threaten boycott of the elections. To reach a compromise, an agreement was reached to cross-check the identity of about 850,000 disputed voters. At the end of the exercise no major changes were made to the list.

The first round of the elections produced no outright winner necessitating a second run. In the first round, Gbagbo, Outarra and Bedie got 38 percent, 32 percent and 25 percent respectively. On 28th November, 2010, the second round of the Presidential elections was held. Four days later the Ivory Coast Elections Commission declared Outarra the winner with 54 percent of the vote. Gbagbo got 46 percent.

Gbagbo's party complained of fraud and ordered the votes from nine regions to be annulled but these claims were refused by the Electoral Commission, and the Constitutional Court, headed by a staunch supporter of Gbagbo, nullified the Electoral Commission and declared Gbagbo the winner with 51 percent of the votes. The constitutional restriction for Presidents not to run for more than two terms was not addressed. Tensions arose. Gbagbo refused to step down when his challenger, Allasane Outarra was internationally recognized as the winner of the elections. The US, African Union and EU recognized Mr. Outtara as the legitimate winner of the elections. Both men had themselves sworn in as Presidents. Ivory Coast now had two Presidents at the same time.

Gbagbo ordered the Army to close borders, and foreign news organizations were banned from within the country. Gbagbo declared, "I will continue to work with all the leaders of the world, but I will never give up our sovereignty." He saw the importance of his continued rule because he said, "Ivory Coast is a nation blessed by God and neo-colonialists want to control it for its cocoa and oil fields." His role was to defend the country from these invaders.

The International Community demanded Gbagbo to cede power. Gbagbo responded by launching ethnic attacks on Northerners living in Abidjan. When Nigeria demanded Gbagbo to step down, and when the EU imposed sanctions and froze his assets, Gbagbo responded by demanding foreign troops, by which he meant the UN and the French troops, to leave the country. Mr. Gbagbo's wife, Simone is a powerful politician in her own right and many suspect that she took an active role in persuading Gbagbo not to give up power.

Gbagbo was arrested on 11 April. Speaking from his place of custody, he told his supporters to stop fighting. Three thousand people had perished in the feud. United States President, Barack Obama, cheered the news, saying Gbagbo's capture "sends a strong signal to dictators and tyrants that . . . they may not disregard the voice of their own people."

Rough road ahead

According to Ogwang (2011:1), the conflict in Ivory Coast is a by-product of deep seated cleavages revolving around ethnicity, nationality and religion. Politicians tapped into these differences to consolidate their monopoly of power and in the process pushed the country towards civil war. Against this background, Alassane Outarra has inherited a deeply divided country and peace in the country will largely depend on how he approaches the process of building the differences in the Ivorian society. As Outtara owes his rise to power to the loose coalition of Northern rebel groups who might demand a role in government, this complicates the already complex situation.

In short, the system that Alassane Outtara has inherited is the same that produced the leadership of Robert Guie and Laurent Gbagbo. In the absence of a high level of consciousness, the system could potentially turn Outarra into the same type of leader that Gbagbo and Guie were. Hope lies in the capacity and willingness to identify, surface and confront contradictions in the system in the effort to align the system to the hopes and aspirations of all Ivorians.

4. Uganda—Yoweri Museveni

My introduction to Uganda

My first trip outside Africa was in December, 1999 when I was invited by the World Bank to present a paper I entitled "Challenges Facing NGOs in Africa and the Role of Organization Development in addressing them." In the opening session of the conference, the keynote speaker was Professor Appolo Nsibambi, Prime Minister of Uganda. I cannot remember much of what he said but I was particularly impressed when he said his journey had been so long and by the time he arrived he was so tired and had developed a headache. To relieve the pain, he said, he took, "some Western pain killer tablets and a few African (Ugandan) herbs." He was trying to emphasize the point that *knowledge is like a baobab tree; no one person can embrace it all alone.* In other words, Northern and Southern knowledge must complement each other in contrast to the current dominance of Northern (European and American) knowledge on the market. He was trying to say that development must have "two legs"—one local, the other international, and the need to balance the two for synergy.

Towards the end of the conference I was in the same group with the Prime Minister discussing how to take the outputs of the conference forward as Africans. We exchanged a few pleasantries and he gave me his card. "When you come to Uganda, please call me," he said, I presume jokingly, "and I will send you my official convoy to come and pick you up."

Unfortunately, the chance for me to visit Uganda never came until 2005. I made some effort to book an appointment through his office but it did not yield anything. I later realized that early 2006 was going to be an election year and probably he was very busy; and being a busy man he had probably forgotten about me.

This was my introduction to Uganda. I stayed in Uganda, intermittently for nine months and totally fell in love with the country. I made it a point, as much as possible to visit at least once a year from that year.

A brief history

President Yoweri Kaguta Museveni was born in 1944. He has been President of Uganda since 1986. He studied economics and political science in Dar es Salaam University. While in college, he became a Marxist, involving himself in radical pan-African politics. He studied under the eminent leftist Walter Rodney. He wrote his thesis on the applicability of Fran Fanon's ideas of revolutionary violence to post-colonial Africa. Mr. Museveni was involved in the deposing of the legendary dictator, Idi Amin Dada. He later ousted Dr. Obote and became President.

On May 12, 1996, Museveni began his second term in office after defeating Mohammed Mayanja Kibirige and Paul Semogerere. Mr. Museveni's campaign was a promise for restoration of security and economic normality to much of the country. The other candidates could not match his efficacy in communication and connection power with the people, and he easily sailed through.

In 2001 Mr. Museveni beat Dr. Kizza Besigye with 69 percent of the votes. Dr Besigye petitioned the court, claiming that the elections were not free and fair. The court agreed but declined to nullify the outcome by a 3:2 decision.

In 2006, Mr. Museveni, again beat Dr. Besigye with 59 percent of the votes. There was more evidence of malpractice this time but the court upheld the results by a 4:3 decision.

A New dawn for Uganda

Mr. Museveni's party, the National Resistance Movement (NRM) inherited a heavily fragmented country destroyed by the dictatorships of Idi Amin Dada and Dr. Milton Obote. He inherited decades of government mistrust, rebel activity and civil war. Mr. Museveni undertook to clean house from top to bottom and ushered in a period of steady reform and economic growth. The NRM developed a 10-point plan to bring about major reforms in Uganda. The plan covered key areas of "democracy, security, consolidation of national unity, deepening national independence, building an independent and self-sustaining economy, improvement of social services, elimination of corruption and misuse of power, redressing inequality and cooperation with other African countries as key priorities."

The economy that had been damaged by the civil war began to recover as Mr. Museveni initiated economic policies designed to combat key problems such as hyper inflation and the balance of payments. He abandoned his Marxist ideals and embraced the World Bank and IMF structural adjustment initiatives. By the year 2000 Uganda had become the first African country to revert to the per capita income enjoyed in 1970s. In addition Uganda introduced a comprehensive Health program to fight the HIV and AIDS pandemic. Uganda was also the first country to have significantly reduced infection levels nation-wide (Calderisi, 2007: 161).

As early as the 1990s, President Museveni was praised by the West as one of the "new generation of African leaders." The *New York Times* in 1997 said of him,

> These are heady days for the former guerrilla who runs Uganda. He moves with a measured gait and sure gestures of a leader secure in his power and his vision. It is little wonder to hear some of the diplomats and African experts tell it, President Yoweri Museveni's stated ideological movement that is shaping much of Africa, spelling the end of the corrupt, strong man governments that characterized the cold war era. These days, political pundits across the continent are calling Mr. Museveni an African Bismarck. Some people now refer to him as Africa's other statesman, second only to the venerated South African President, Nelson Mandela.

A dimming vision

A number of events have progressively contributed to the dimming of the "Uganda miracle." In October, 2010, a leaked document for the US ambassador in Uganda read, "President Museveni's autocratic tendencies, as well as Uganda's pervasive corruption, sharpening ethnic division and explosive population growth, are eroding Uganda's status as an African success story."

The 1995 Uganda constitution provided for a two five-year Presidential limit. Given Uganda's history of dictatorial regimes, this was meant to prevent monopolization of power by a long serving leader in what was dubbed "the life Presidency project" by the opposition Forum for Democratic Change (FDC). There were claims of buying MPs to vote in favor of the bill. President Museveni sacked key influential supporters and friends deemed not to be towing the Presidential line. Commenting on the process, the FDC observed:

> The country is polarized with many Ugandans objecting to the constitutional amendments. If parliament goes ahead and removes the Presidential term limit, this may cause serious unrest, political strife and may lead to turmoil both through the transition period and thereafter . . . we would like to appeal to President Museveni to respect himself, the people who elected him and the Constitution under which he was voted President in 2001 when he promised the world at large to hand over power peacefully and in an orderly manner at the end of his second and last term. His insistence to stand again will expose him as a consummate liar and biggest political fraudster this country has ever known (James McKinley; *New York Times*, 5 June, 1997).

President Museveni responded to the mounting pressure by accusing donors of meddling in internal politics and using aid to manipulate poor countries. Despite many local and international calls to dissuade Mr. Museveni to abandon his campaign, he went ahead to change the constitution.

In 2009, Mr. Museveni refused Kabaka Mwenda Mutebi, the Buganda king, permission to visit Kayunga which is part of his kingdom. Riots ensued and some people were killed, others injured. A number of people were arrested. Some people termed Museveni's third term as his "sad term" rhyming it with Uganda's pronunciation of the word "third."

Whither Uganda?

Mr. Museveni's fourth term in office as President began in February 2011 after, again beating Dr. Kizza Besigye with a very wide margin of 68 percent. The election results were disputed by both European Union and the opposition. The electoral process was marred with avoidable administrative and logistical failures, according to the European Union electoral observers team.

Two months after Mr. Museveni's fourth re-election, continuous protests swept Kampala and across the nation because of "increasing inflation of prices of things and they are treating Dr. Kizza Besigye badly" as one little Ugandan girl told me. At least about 10 people were killed. The protests were mostly due to rising fuel and cost of living. However, Mr. John Nagenda, advisor to President Museveni, said on BBC Network Africa of 28th June, 2011, the real motive for the protests was Mr. Besigye's frustration to losing the elections and his promise to make Uganda ungovernable as a result.

Two months later, the governor of the Reserve Bank of Uganda accused President Museveni of excessive spending and of "following Marxist approaches." The President purchased fighter jets at the cost of $740 million. Most of the people felt this was not a wise way of using such a huge amount of money given the challenges people were facing and the complaints they had about rising cost of living. Mr. John Nagenda said national security was a more important priority to government. As a result a number of donors reduced their budgetary support to Uganda and the countries import cover dropped from six to four months. Mr. Nagenda said government was not worried with the reduced support from the donors as Uganda would be able to earn $4billion within three years from the oil that had just been discovered in the country.

During the protests, key opposition leaders were arrested and often released on bail. Mr. Museveni said the protests were a "political insurrection" and that one of the priorities of his party in parliament would be to pass a bill forbidding anyone arrested on these issues to be given bail for at least six months (BBC Focus on Africa, 10 May, 2011).

In response to local and international criticism at his long stay in power, Mr. Museveni argues that he should be judged not by the time he has spent in power but by what he has been able to do. He promised to, in the fourth term; transform Uganda into a middle class income country using revenues from the newly discovered oil which was expected to start drilling within two years. He also said, he would make up his mind in consultation with the NRM on whether to run for a fifth term in 2016 or not. Mr. Museveni says his wish before leaving power is the realization of the East African Political Federation. He argues that if the political federation is realized by the five East African countries of Uganda, Kenya, Tanzania, Rwanda and Burundi, he would happily go home and comfortably look after his cows.

President Museveni's critics see him as having failed in fighting corruption which they say has gripped his government. Mr. Museveni says fighting corruption is going to be one of his main emphasis areas in the fourth term. He also says anti-corruption laws have already been executed to help him fight the vice.

Yoweri Museveni's people love him. They still vote for him but almost three decades in power in the modern world gives Mr. Museveni more negatives than positives. The longer people stay in office the more they believe and the more they are told that they are indispensable. If Mr. Museveni left power after two terms in office, he would have left a very strong legacy as a great African statesman.

5. Rwanda—Paul Kagame

A brief background

Rwanda is the most densely populated African country. Its population density is three times that of Nigeria, Africa's most populous nation; and ten times that of neighboring Tanzania. The population of Rwanda, like that of neighboring Burundi comprises two major ethnic groups (the Hutus who comprise 85 percent and the Tutsis who comprise 15 percent). The Hutus are primarily farmers while the Tutsis are mostly pastoralists.

Rwanda became independent in 1962. Soon after the independence the Hutus were already agitating to overthrow the Tutsis from leadership. In the next two decades up to a million Tutsis fled the country as the Hutus gained the upper hand. In 1973, a Hutu general, Habyarimana staged a coup against the Tutsi-dominated government and succeeded.

Habyarimana was accommodative to the Tutsis and ensured that there was peace between the two ethnic groups. He brought stability to the country and brought it to notable levels of progress and prosperity for 15 years. The country, however, met a setback because of declining prices of tea and coffee, Rwanda's main cash crops on the international market in 1989 coupled with some droughts and cumulative environmental challenges arising mainly from deforestation, soil erosion and loss of soil fertility.

In 1990 a civil war broke out which displaced about one million Rwandese into settlement camps. In 1993, a peace agreement was agreed in Arusha for a power sharing government. Some business men and close colleagues were not happy with the power sharing government and decided to "revenge" on the Tutsis in the country as there were regular Tutsi invasions from neighboring countries; and in neighboring Burundi there were reports of Tutsis killing Hutus. They bought machetes and distributed them to militia men and began to train them in preparation.

A spark to the genocide was the downing of Habyarimana's plane at Kigali Airport on 6 April 1994. He was traveling together with the President of Burundi. Both Presidents (including all on board) perished. The perpetrators of the act have not been identified up to now. But it is clear that he had many enemies both among the Tutsis and fellow Hutus who thought he was too soft to the Tutsis.

Within an hour of the downing of the plane, the Hutu militia killed the Tutsi Prime Minister and proceeded to eliminate all in the Hutu leadership who were deemed too sympathetic to the Tutsis. With internal opposition removed, they took over government and used the radio to coordinate national cleansing of the Tutsis. Soldiers, Hutu civilians and even some priests of the Catholic Church took part in the killing. They used guns, machetes and clubs to kill the Tutsis. Women's breasts were chopped off, limbs were cut off and children were thrown into wells and there was wide spread rape. Within six weeks, an estimated 800,000 Tutsi's out of their population of one million had been killed.

Kagame's group, the Rwanda Patriotic Front (RPF), coming from Uganda fought the Hutu extremist government and ousted it from power on July 18, 1994. That ended the genocide and, RPF, the Tutsi rebel group took over power. The new government emphasized reconciliation and unity; and encouraged solidarity and national consciousness. About 2 million Hutus fled into exile and about 750,000 former exiles, especially, Tutsis returned to Rwanda.

Jared Diamond convincingly argues that political factors aside, population pressure leading to smaller and smaller allocation of available land to especially poor people coupled with diminishing opportunities were the major contributors to the genocide in Rwanda. He says,

> Severe problems of overpopulation, environmental impact and climate change cannot persist indefinitely; soon or later they are likely to resolve themselves whether in the manner of Rwanda or some other manner not of our own devising, if we do not succeed in resolving them by our actions (2005: 328).

This means that preventing a similar catastrophe from happening again in the future must consciously include looking into and addressing these deeper issues.

Paul Kagame was born on 23rd October, 1957. In 1960, at the age of two he left with his parents for Uganda where he grew up. He joined the Ugandan army. He rose to the rank of head of military intelligence in the NRA and was regarded as one of Museveni's closest allies. He formed the Rwandan Patriotic Front in 1985. He went for military training at Fort Leavenworth, in the US in 1990. He got further military training from the UK. Kagame's Rwandan Patriotic Front got training in counter insurgency and combat from US Special Forces. This training was put to use in the 1996–1997 Rwanda backed military campaigns to overthrow the government of the Republic of Zaire.

Presidency

Kagame became President of Rwanda in 2000 after Bizimungu was deposed. Kagame, like Museveni, were widely regarded as a new generation of African leadership. In 2003, he won a landslide victory in the first national elections with 99.5 percent of the votes. Kagame is credited with ending the infamous Rwanda genocide. Under his leadership, Rwanda has been called Africa's biggest success story. He is an advocate of new models of foreign aid designed to help recipients to become more self reliant. In 2011, Kagame won a landslide victory of 99% for another seven year term.

Kagame is very critical of the United Nations and its role in the 1994 genocide. In March, 2004, his public criticism of France for its role in the genocide and its lack of preventive actions caused a diplomatic row. In 2006, Rwanda cut all diplomatic ties with France and ordered all French diplomatic staff out of Rwanda within 24 hours following a French judges issuing warrants accusing nine high ranking Rwandans of plotting the downing of President Juvenile Habyarimana's plane in 1994; and also accusing Kagame of ordering shooting down of the plane.

Kagame is critical of the West's genuine interest in seeing a developed Africa. He believes Western countries deliberately keep African products out of the World market place. He praises China as bringing a better alternative, "investment and money for governments and companies."

Kagame has and continues to receive numerous accolades. Some of these include:

- The 2003 Global Leadership Award in recognition to his "commitment and tireless work to address crises, to foster understanding, unity and peace to the benefit of all people." This was awarded by the Young President's Association.

- An honorary doctor of law degree by the University of the Pacific in the US in 2005
- Andrew Young Medal for Capitalism and Social Progress by George Washington University in the US, 2005
- African National Achievement Award by the Africa America Institute in the US in 2005
- Honorary doctorate degree, Oklahoma Christian University, USA, 2006
- 2006 ICT Africa Award in 2006
- In September, 2006, Rwanda was listed as a top 10 reformer of the ease of doing business index by the World Bank
- In July, 2007, Kagame was given the Hands off Cain Award for his role in ending the death penalty in his country.
- In November, 2007, Kagame was awarded an honorary degree of doctor of Law by the University of Glasgow in Scotland.
- In December, 2007, Kagame was given the Africa Gender Award in Dakar, Senegal for his role in promoting gender in Rwanda.
- In March, 2009, Kagame was awarded The Distinction of the Grand Cerdon in the Most Venerable Order of the Knighthood of Pioneers by Liberia's President Ellen Johnson Sirleaf. This is the highest honor in Liberia. It was given to Kagame in recognition of his exemplary leadership and exceptional contribution to the promotion of women rights.
- In June, 2009, Kagame was awarded the Children's Champion Award by the UN Fund for Children (UNICEF) for promoting children rights.
- In September, 2009, he was awarded the International Peace Model from the Saddleback Church for his support and role in the P.E.A.C.E plan.
- In September, 2009, Kagame was honoured with the Clinton Global Citizen Award in recognition of his leadership in the public service that has improved the lives of the people of Rwanda.
- In November, 2009, Kagame was presented with the Most Innovative People Award for Economic Innovation at the Lebanon 2020 Summit.
- In May, 2010, Kagame was awarded the life time Leadership Award for Development and Equality by the Rwanda Women in recognition of his efforts in developing the nation and promoting equality among Rwandans.
- In May 2010, Kagame was awarded the 2010 Rwanda Convention Association Award of Excellence in recognition of his role in steering Rwanda towards a knowledge based economy and promotion of the private sector.
- On June 5, 2010 Kagame was awarded the prestigious Energy Globe Award on the Occasion of the World Environment Day celebrated in Kigali, Rwanda.

- On July 5, 2010 the Rwanda International Network Association (RINA) awarded Kagame for his continuous efforts in promotion of education.
- On September 27, 2010 the British Magazine, *New Statesman*, included Paul Kagame in its list of the world's 50 most influential figures in 2010 on the 49th place.
- On November 19, 2010, Kagame was presented the Grand Croix—order de merit du Benin, the country's highest national award. This award is awarded exclusively to personalities of the rank of head of state in recognition of outstanding achievements to express esteem.

This is as of the end of 2010. In 2011 and the years to come more and more awards are sure to come.

Accusations

Kagame's government is highly criticized for poor human rights record. His police have been accused of several instances of extra-judicial killings and deaths in custody. There have been allegations of serious violations of international humanitarian law committed by the Rwanda Patriotic Front.

There are reports that Kagame allows less political space and press freedom at home than Robert Mugabe does in Zimbabwe. Anyone posing the slightest political threat is dealt with ruthlessly. The United States Government in 2006 described Rwanda's human rights record as mediocre, citing disappearances of political dissidents as well as arbitrary arrests and acts of violence, torture and murders committed by the police.

In 2007, Reporters without Borders ranked Rwanda 147 out of 169 countries for freedom of press. They also reported that Rwandan journalists suffer permanent hostility from the government and surveillance by the security services. The report cited cases of journalists being threatened, harassed and arrested for criticizing government. The report also asserts that President Kagame and his government have never accepted that the press should be granted genuine freedom.

Political marginalization of the majority of the Rwandans who survived the genocide—most of them remain extremely poor, in need of food, clean water and affordable proximate health services. This is mostly for the people living in the rural areas who are in the majority. On the other hand, the few living in urban areas enjoy high levels of "modern life" including coffee houses, wireless internet hotspots, new housing and shopping malls, and accessible health care. The gap between the rural citizens comprising 90% of the population and the urban elite has never been larger as it is today.

The population continues to grow with estimates that in 2020 the population will be 13 million up from 11 million in 2011, making Rwanda the most densely populated country in Africa with 225 people per square mile. This will further increase pressure on land and as of now Kagame's government does not allow peasant farmers to voice concern about agricultural policies and the inequitable distribution of land among government loyalists.

There is a need for more engagement with diverse political views especially with the Rwandan Diaspora. The people in the Diaspora are a major force and cannot be treated as though they do not exist. In 2010 Rwanda received $130 million in remittances, an amount second only to tourism. Well meaning opponents who question government policy are lumped with political extremists or fundamentalist which makes it easy to exclude them from the Rwanda political landscape.

Many educated and urban people, mostly those who came back after the 1994 genocide feel apathetic and fatalistic. They have lost faith in the vision and reconstruction efforts of the government. They generally consider the government corrupt and nepotistic. Several military officers feel the same.

Adam Hochschild (2011) in a *New York Times* book review of Jason Stearn's book, *Dancing in the Glory of Monsters*, noted, "How this media savvy autocrat (Kagame) has managed to convince so many American journalists, diplomats and political leaders that he is a great statesman is worth a book in itself." Some observers (Diamond, 2006 and Thomson, 2011) are warning that the current leadership in Rwanda has not dealt adequately with the issues or root causes that led to the 1994 genocide. They observe that if the current developments in Rwanda are not checked, there are fears that Rwanda could be setting the stage for the next genocide.

Conclusion

Writing in 1971, Babu (Rodney, 1971: 287) noted, "With all due respect, it is difficult to imagine, apart from one or two honorable exceptions, any of the present African leaders who is capable of standing up for the genuine rights of his people, knowing that these rights are of necessity directly opposed to the interests of imperialism." Much earlier than that, in the early 1920s, a report on Liberia concerning the leaders or Americo-Liberians recorded, "They were the ruling class and although educated, constitute the most despicable element in Liberia . . . To any man who can read and write there is but one goal: a government office, where he can graft." The report further observed that the love of liberty may have brought the African Americans to Liberia but they had not extended those rights to the local indigenous population. The African Americans had 'fled' a slave system and transplanted much of the master/servant ethos to their new found land. The report further observed the visible lack of progress and development as a result of the bad leadership. There was obvious large scale misappropriation of funds; there was not a mile of road in all of Liberia, and in Monrovia not a street worthy a name. Bush grew in front and around executive mansions. Despite all this the average Liberian was as proud as a peacock and boasted that at least they were no longer slaves in America (Grant, 2009:280).

It is sad to say that today, after so many years, much of the going observations still ring true. In the case of protecting the people against imperialism, what is worse now is that the rights of the people are often not of necessity directly opposed to the interests of imperialism only but more importantly to those of their own leaders. This is a sure testimony that the system which was operating in the 1920s in Liberia and 1971 in Africa is still alive and well today.

The behavior of many African leaders is giving more ground to those who believe that Africans are not capable, at least for now, to govern themselves.

The similarities in issues in the five profiles unravel something that makes one's hair stands on end: the exploits of all the five leaders seem to suggest they suckled from the same breast, brothers from one mother. The mother in this case is the system. As long as the system is in place, it will churn one of its kind. Unless there is an overhaul of this system, we should forget about genuine change no matter the person in office. Key characteristics of this system and leadership include broken visions and promises, nepotism and tribalism, mediocrity, lies, personality cult, concentration of power and tendency to overstay in office; and above all, a promotion of a culture of fear. These characteristics are from the DNA of animal farm systems.

CHAPTER 5: THE MARKS OF ANIMAL FARM SYSTEMS

Introduction

This chapter draws parallels between the Animal Farm story and the African leaders discussed in the previous chapter (and African leaders in general). The aim is to pinpoint similarities and where possible, differences. The chapter tries to prove that the two stories, one from the animal farm book and the other from the stories of the presidents, are mostly one and the same.

The perfect picture of the first African leaders is that of a crop of masters of animal farm systems, systems they inherited from colonial masters, systems they in turn perfected for their own ends. Nkrumah, Nasser, Senghor, Houphouet Boigny, Sekou Toure, Keita, Olympio, Kenyatta, Nyerere, Kaunda and Banda, all enjoyed a lot of prestige and honor, and were perceived to personify the states they led. That being not enough for them, they quickly consolidated their control by seeking a monopoly of power, establishing a system of personal rule, instilling fear, and encouraging personality cults. They were seen to be and they believed that they were specially elected by God to rule their people (Meredith 2006:162). The irony is that it was the African nationalists exiled by colonial administrations to the barren African bush or tortured in infamous colonial prisons who became despots after independence, intolerant of multiparty politics, preferring to imprison, exile or even kill their political opponents, writers, journalists, lawyers, musicians, radical thinkers and other rebels, instead of accommodating them within the fabric of their liberated societies (Mapanje, 2002: xvi–xvii). Mapanje (2002: xvii) further observes that in Kenya for example, after the Mau Mau struggle had led the country to independence, it was Jomo Kenyatta himself who began to hunt down the Mau Mau fighters who were dissatisfied with his rule, calling them "these evil men, vagrants."

The sad thing is that, among most African leaders today, while some changes are perceptible, no fundamental shift away from this attitude has occurred. Cammack (2009: 153) gives a tacit observation of this: "The culture is so strong that political idealists are elected and then behave like the old politicians they once castigated."

Broken visions and promises

Animal farm leaders often replace very bad regimes that people are tired with. Sometimes people vote them in "just to see something different as they are fed up with the current regime." Many times, however, people welcome them as saviors as they bring visions of hope, a sense of a break from the past.

It is important to note that politicians are seemingly more intelligent and objective when they are outside government. Once they get in the story is often different. Even Idi Amin Dada, the Ugandan legendary tyrant, speaking in exile from his home in Saudi Arabia said, "What Uganda needs is democracy. Of course, I can see that democracy would not work immediately in Uganda. Security is very bad there now, and there are many problems. Democracy takes discipline. But a tough person with military knowledge like me could teach the people discipline and prepare them for democracy" (Lamb, 1987: 345).

Some of the leaders have good intentions but once in power they fall prey to the common weakness of lack of preparation for leadership through self development and development of a personal philosophy upon which one builds one's convictions. Because of this shortfall, they soon fall prey to the trappings of power. Nasser (1955: 9) observes that the person who can master corruption without being corrupted, can wield power without installing tyranny and can master events without losing his soul, is a hero in history. Well meaning African leaders have set out to conquer corruption only to be corrupted themselves, making it necessary for them to install tyranny and to sell their souls just to keep on in power. Some have gone to extreme cases of keeping in power by killing as many people as possible. These are leaders who turn to oppression to remain in power.

Most of the current crop of African leaders does not have a testimony of their personal "process of becoming a leader." In other words, they are leaders by accident. All true leaders including Marcus Garvey, Malcolm X, Barack Obama and Nelson Mandela, as examples, have clear and convincing stories about their personal journey and evolution to become leaders even before they became prominent figures.

A leader who does not have a strong foundation for leadership cannot survive the temptations of leadership for long. With great power comes great responsibility. The aspect of genuine responsibility misses in many leaders. One's sense of responsibility is based on one's foundation of self development. Leaders may come up with impressive visions and promises but soon or later their shortfalls of lack of a leadership foundation will begin to catch up with them. True colors will begin to emerge and overtake them. This is too common a story in many African countries.

Finding a solution is complicated because the opposition, which has just been ousted from power, has no legitimacy to speak out since it is for the very same reasons they were booted out. Too many times civil society organizations become complacent after a long and tiring battle in ousting the party which is now in opposition. This situation creates too much space for the new regime as the checks and balances are minimal. This creates a conducive environment for corruption and other forms of bad governance to breed, and with time, entrench themselves as part of "bad governance."

Animal farm systems do not get corrupted overnight. The process is gradual. Many times by the time people realize what is happening, it is almost too late. In all the countries mentioned in the last chapter, the coming of the new leaders signified the beginning of the new era, but this feeling was always short-lived. Within a few years, people began to notice that their hope was misplaced. Same vices they had fought against in regimes since ousted began to resurface. Mandela (2010: 406) observes that

> history never stops to play tricks even with seasoned and world famous freedom fighters. Frequently, erstwhile revolutionaries have easily succumbed to greed and the tendency to divert public resources for personal enrichment. By amassing vast personal wealth and by betraying the noble objectives which made them famous, they virtually deserted the masses of the people and joined

> the former oppressors, who enriched themselves by mercilessly robbing the poorest of the poor.

Freedom fighters that later desert their people is the essence of the story of Animal Farm. The animal farm systems eventually drop their well meaning vision and promise and begin to run the country only for today and only for themselves. They are like the stupid animals in Animal farm that were asking why they should worry and care about what will happen to "those who come after us when we are dead." These leaders refuse to accept the fact of their mortality and somehow believe that they will be leaders in the same positions of power forever despite the fact that most of them are already in the evenings of their lives. All constitutional changes are made to serve such self-interests.

Mr. Frederick Chiluba, former President of Zambia, was hailed as a new brand of leaders on the African continent, replacing autocratic old guards after defeating Kenneth Kaunda in 1991. When he came into office he was hailed as Zambia's "liberator." He won praise for his economic and political reforms. Under Chiluba Zambia was considered a model of African democracy.

However, towards the end of his ten year rule, he was accused of embezzlement and turning a blind eye to corruption, especially among his cronies. He was also accused of taking an authoritarian approach to his political opponents, firing critical colleagues and jailing outspoken journalists. He attempted to change the constitution so that he could run for a third term in office. He only gave up after massive public protests. In 2007, he was convicted, in a UK court, of fraud and asked to pay back $58 million to the government of Zambia. The ruling was never carried out in Zambia.

A self-confessed born again Christian and preacher, Mr Chiluba' legacy is one of the many sad stories of African leaders. He inherited the system left behind by President Kenneth Kaunda and left it intact if not worse as far as the culture of embezzlement is concerned. He did not bring any fundamental transformation to the system. Either he failed to change it or the system changed him for the worse. Because of the gross contradictions in his leadership, his intended Frederick Chiluba Center for Democracy and Good Governance became a joke and it never took off.

Another example is that of Mr. Robert Mugabe of Zimbabwe. Lamb (1987: 334) wrote,

> Mugabe, a disciplined scholar and non-practicing Catholic spent ten years in detention or under restriction until 1974 in Rhodesia and the whites greatest fear was that he would persecute his former tormenters, turn Zimbabwe into a communist state aligned with Moscow and preside over the disintegration of another African economy. None of those things happened, and Mugabe has shown far more respect for the due process of law than Ian Smith ever did. As the elected Prime Minister, Mugabe wisely juggled black hopes and white fears and the process proved him to be perhaps the most capable leader in black Africa.

Today, it is almost unbelievable that this statement was ever written.

Despite being very highly educated, most African leaders do not demonstrate that their education and exposure have added value to their leadership and leadership styles. Four of the five leaders in the previous chapter have doctorate degrees and sometimes more than one. This seems to prove the point: degrees do not make a man. It is conscious self development and experiences that make a man or a woman. The toughest work in an individual's life is to know and master oneself. Without conscious and continuous self development it is not possible to change oneself—the most critical prerequisite to changing animal farm systems.

The shadow of extended families in Africa

The African extended family has many merits, no question about it, but the African extended family usually plays accomplice to animal farm systems. For change to happen people must have enough motivation and they must pass through a threshold of pain. Africans rarely experience death or life situations because they can always fall back on the extended family for economic support. Africans passively accept the downward mobility arising from state failure because they know that they have an alternative source of the services or the opportunities which is the extended family. The extended family is a key distinguishing factor between African and other family systems in Europe and America. In a Western setting the nuclear family consists of the husband, wife and children. In Africa a family consists of all the people who are directly and indirectly connected by blood and marriage. It includes all the living, the dead and the unborn. A key characteristic of the family is that it shares everything and everyone is entitled. Those who have more have to share with those who do not have. This includes sharing money, services and opportunities.

Poor people depend on and put pressure on better off relatives rather than put it on government or the state. As a result, the state does not feel the full weight of its obligations to the citizens. There is a social contract between the state and the citizens (and that's the reason we conduct elections—to legitimize this contract), a contract of rights and obligations. The basis of the social contract is the constitution. A key responsibility of every citizen is to know the constitution and to defend it from being manipulated and changed in the interest of animal farm system leaders.

The state has obligations towards the citizens, key of which are provision of services and an enabling environment for them to make progress in their different endeavors without which development is impossible. The obligations of the state are the rights of the citizens. If this is fulfilled, the government gets the right of legitimacy, in the honest sense of the word, from the citizenry.

The obligations of the citizens are to make sure that the state is discharging its obligations and if not to give pressure until the state is able to do so or withdraw the legitimacy given to the state so it should step down to allow other more capable leaders to take over legitimately.

A key hindrance to national development in Africa is that citizens do not look up to the state for provision of services and an enabling environment, but rather they look up to the extended family. In this way, the extended family seems to replace the state. And it is also through this that the state is let off the hook, and from the pressure from the citizens. Put simply, the citizens have an easier alternative: the extended family. They do not feel the need to fight for their rights for services and an e enabling environment from the state when the extended family can provide the same. In fact, they do not recognize that in the modern setting, the reason we have the state is to take away the economic responsibilities from the extended family to the state. And that their first port of call must be the state before turning to the extended family. This is why taxes are paid. In normal settings, when government fails to provide services or to create an enabling environment for the people to pursue such goals as getting employed, the state is under obligation to put all those citizens under social welfare—to provide money to ensure that the population can afford a basic living.

As long as people cannot see things in this light and they keep going back to the extended family for "services and an enabling environment," the state in Africa will always be let off the hook and will not feel the need or pressure to meet its obligations towards the citizens. True national citizenship means that people have shifted their primary dependency on services and creation of an enabling environment from the extended family to the state. In a modern state, the primary role of the extended family is to be a social support system, not an economic support system. It is the role of the state to be an economic support system. As long as extended family systems are driven by dependency rather than interdependency, poverty will never go away as we cannot eliminate poverty by distributing it within ourselves.

Nepotism

Animal farm systems are also characterized by nepotism in which privileges and positions are given based on closeness to the leader either through blood or otherwise and not based on merit. In some countries, key civil and public sector positions are conspicuously taken by people of one tribe—the ethnic tribe of the President. In countries led by former freedom fighters one observes that positions are given to reward those who were involved in the struggle, many a time rewarding incompetence.

In responding to a situation in which the Muslims were demanding a certain percentage of jobs to be preserved for them, irrespective of qualifications, because the Christians and Hindus had the advantage of better education and connections, Mahatma Gandhi (Fischer, 1997: 279) replied:

> For administration to be efficient it must be in the hands of the fittest. There should certainly be no favoritism. If we want five engineers we must not take one from each community but we must take the fittest even if they were all Muslims or Parsis . . . those who aspire to occupy responsible posts in the government of the country can only do so if they pass the required test.

One of the consequences of nepotism and appeasement policy is over-bloated cabinets and too many members of parliament. Ruling parties will continue to create more and more constituencies in areas where they are strong with the aim of increasing numerical strength in parliament. In many African countries there are too many ministries, sometimes to the point of duplicating duties. In addition, to having too many ministries, one also observes that there are too many deputy ministers whose job descriptions sometimes leaves a lot to be desired. This negatively impacts on the tax payers' money.

Related to nepotism one also observes that there are selective punitive actions on wrong doers. Many times those within the circle of the leader are above the law. They can break the law with impunity while the slightest offences of the others are given the harshest treatment. In many countries anti-corruption institutions are toothless bulldogs in the presence of sacred bulls.

Mediocrity

Singapore is one of the few countries that have shown how a country can move from a typical third world country to a first world country within a generation. Their formula is not a secret. Singapore followed a trade rather than aid route by linking up with the developed world—America, Europe and Japan; and attracting their manufacturers to produce in Singapore and export their products to the developed countries. In order to get the manufacturers to Singapore, they set out to make Singapore a first World Oasis in a Third World Region by changing Third World habits into First World standards of service (Lee, 2000:57–58).

The difference between Singapore and African countries is that the leaders in Singapore walked their talk. Their attitude was "we will make it happen no matter what it costs even to our own personal interests." As Mills (2010: 149) has observed, a key weakness among African leaders is that they have "cherry picked" the lessons from success stories like the one from Singapore. They take the juicy segments and avoid the less digestible bits. They have a tendency to replicate structure and process and not the mindset behind the success stories. A key mindset issue is to allow robust debate around the proposed plans and ability to take in opinions that we may not like but which look more sensible than our own. The failure to receive critical feedback turns most projects in Africa into white elephants.

Success requires fierce arguments on key issues to ensure that agreed propositions have been scrutinized and looked over from all angles. This was one of Napoleon's biggest weaknesses in *Animal Farm*: the desire to get all credit to him and to look like the one, all-knowing. It is not possible to copy success without engaging in the deep, complex issues involved especially around the difficult choices to be made and the democracy required in the whole process.

Many leaders in Africa are succeeding today in convincing their people that getting basic services is an impossible task and that the people should just adjust to mediocrity. Many African leaders are convincing their people that getting electricity and running water every day is an impossible task. They are convincing their people that getting fuel without queuing for days is an impossible task. They are convincing their people that buying fish, meat and other basic food stuffs is only possible for the rich. They are convincing their people that government hospitals are not supposed to have drugs. Children are born, grow up and get married under these circumstance and since it is the only life they have known, it is settled in their minds that the leaders are right. Most

Africans have come to accept that their lot in life is to play junior partners at the global stage. They believe this is destiny's portion for them. There is a great need to change this political culture and mindset.

Most poor people today are living by the "grace of God" not in the religious sense but in a literal sense. One of the greatest pains of being poor is to see your child die from a curable disease simply because the hospital has no medicine and that you cannot afford to buy the medicine if it was there. It is very painful to lose a loved one who dies because the electricity went out when he was being operated on and there was no diesel in the generator.

Mediocrity is also related to a poor foundation in one's leadership. A person must go through a process which I call the baptism of leadership at some critical stage in their life before taking on serious leadership responsibilities. This is usually in the form of some intensive period of introspection and self discovery. It is during this period that the individual forms their personal vision of how the world could be and the needed disciplines on how they can build themselves up to rise to the level of the vision. This is the foundation that gives one unshakeable convictions. It is also the foundation upon which the individual builds their leadership philosophy for life. This is the foundation that prepares the individual for their purpose in life. It is the baptism of leadership that enables the individual to conquer mediocrity and the universal human natural propensity to seek power for personal wealth and recognition rather than for conscious contribution to humanity.

A person enters into the baptism as an ordinary individual and comes out as a true leader. It is this baptism that gives the individual their testimony of leadership—the story of how they became a leader. It is the conscious leader who has passed through this process who has enough conviction and strength to conquer mediocrity. It also enables him to face and destroy animal farm systems. Otherwise most accidental leaders, rather than changing the animal farm systems, are changed by the systems they set out to destroy. Without this baptism the best one can hope for is to be just another leader or an "also run."

Economical with truth

The truth is the scarcest commodity among most politicians in Africa. It is a rare politician indeed who will tell his or her people the truth or the hard facts the people need to know. Dr. Malegapuru Makgoba observed that politicians are trained for loyalty and that they get promoted for being economical with truth (Guest, 2005:209). Politicians will emphasize what is going on well and as much as possible avoid what is not going on well. Tyrants always want to paint a rosy picture and give the impression that all is well. They give the impression that they are on track and that they personally are responsible for all the achievements.

A politician in South Africa once declared that all politicians are liars. His statement raised uproar and he was forced to withdraw his statement. But if one takes African politicians as a case, there was much truth in his statement. Animal Farm survived on lies propagated by Squealer. The cases presented in the previous chapter illustrate the broken promises and lies perpetrated by the leaders with the aim of consolidating power to perpetuate their stay in power. In such situations, George Orwell's observation that "in a time of universal deceit telling the truth is a revolutionary act" stands true.

One of the lies by the leaders is that they will "give their people development" when they know full well that one person cannot develop another let alone a country. They can only play their role as facilitators, as development is always self-development. Bad leaders avoid developing this consciousness among the people and as a result many poor people have been manipulated to believe that they should keep them in power because it is only them who have the formula for "development."

In many countries in Africa public media is still heavily censored. The primary aim of the public media is not to inform the people; it is a propaganda vehicle used to manipulate the minds of the uneducated masses that are in the majority, to control their thinking. Lies are sugar-coated to taste as truth especially to the simple-minded masses. There is a strong false belief that if one repeats a lie often enough it becomes politics. Any questioning stance is seen as potential threat and is crushed violently there and then. Animal farm systems assume that it is only the government that is wise enough to know what people need to know. Public media and press publish only the good side and not the bad (Lamb, 1987: 245). It is sad that more than a quarter of a century after this was written, the situation in many African countries remains basically the same. There are a number of private media houses but the public media remains the most dominant in most African countries.

In 1961, the High Court in Lagos found the journalist Chike Obi guilty of sedition as a result of a pamphlet he had published. The pamphlet was entitled "People: The Facts You Must Know." The part deemed seditious read,

> Down with the enemies of the people, the exploiters of the weak and the poor. The days of those who have enriched themselves at the expense of the poor are numbered. The common man in Nigeria can today no longer be fooled by sweet talk at election time only to be exploited and treated like dirt after the booty of office has been shared (Lamb, 1987: 246).

More than fifty years the other side of independence, the practice of exploiting and fooling voters is still very much alive in most countries in Africa. Journalists and writers are still being persecuted and sometimes killed.

Personality cult

An article published on Kwame Nkrumah (Meredith, 2006: 179, 180) read:

> To millions of people living both inside and outside the continent of Africa, Kwame Nkrumah is Africa and Africa is Kwame Nkrumah. When the question was asked: What is going to happen to Africa? It is to one man that everyone looks for the answer: Kwame Nkrumah. To the imperialists and colonialists his name is a curse on their lips; to the settlers his name is a warning that the good old days at the expense of the African are coming to an end; to Africans suffering under foreign domination, his name is a breath of hope and means freedom, brotherhood, and racial equality; to us his people, Kwame Nkrumah is our father, our teacher, our brother, our friend, indeed our very lives, for without him we would no doubt have existed, but we would not have lived.

> There would have been no hope of a cure for our sick souls, no taste of glorious victory after a life time of suffering. What we owe is greater than the air we breathe, for he made us as surely as he made Ghana.

Kwame Nkrumah's titles included Man of Destiny, Star of Africa, His High Dedication and the Redeemer. At the height of the cult of Mobutuism in the 1970s a minister of interior made this declaration:

> In all religions, and at all times, there are prophets. Why not today? God has sent a great prophet, our prestigious Guide Mobutu—this prophet is our liberator, our Messiah. Our Church is the Mouvement Populaire de la Revolution (the ruling party). Its chief is Mobutu, we respect him like one respects a Pope. Our gospel is Mobutuism. This is why the crucifixes must be replaced by the image of our Messiah. And party militants will want to place at its side his glorious mother, Mama Yemo, who gave birth to such a son (Harden, 1990: 37).

Reading the foregoing feels like reading another version of *Animal Farm*'s description of Napoleon. Today, at this hour of time, many African countries still accord their presidents the respect and praise elsewhere reserved for God.

In animal farm systems, politicians, especially of the ruling party are expected or are under obligation to start any interview, address or conversation by first of all thanking the President for his "wise and dynamic leadership." In addition, they are under obligation to thank the President for any success or achievement in the country or in their personal lives. This is generally encouraged among the population as a whole and more especially among party members. Forgetting to do this is an offence usually punishable by loss of position.

There is nothing wrong with thanking the President. What is wrong is making it an obligation to the point that failure to adhere to it warrants punishment. When praise singing is made a culture in a country it undermines the nation's ability for critique and it encourages blind loyalty. It also encourages the attitude of perceiving those in opposition as enemies rather than opponents. One key needed trait on the continent is capacity for critique among followers and capacity to receive constructive feedback among the leaders.

More serious consequences of the culture of praise singing is that leaders are forced to be more economical with the truth as they must say only things that are worthy the praise. This is also one of the factors promoting the use of media to brain-wash the people, to remove in them the gift of critique. This is why animal farm systems are happier where the majority of the population is illiterate and has no capacity for critique.

To understand animal farm systems do not just look at the leader; most importantly look at the people surrounding that leader—whether they are people of integrity or not. Also check whether they are men or women enough to provide critique or even to challenge the leader when he or she is going astray. No matter how good the leader may appear, if he or she is surrounded by sycophants and bootlickers, he or she will soon be corrupted, for it is impossible to be a good leader when surrounded by bad people, people without independent minds. This reminds me of a sarcastic wall hanging I saw in one office which read: "It is better to work alone than work with fools."

Concentration of power

In animal farm systems there is natural propensity to concentrate power in the hands of the leader. Constitutions are continuously changed to give more and more power to the President. Constitutional requirements are regularly violated if they are not convenient to the President. There are usually blurred boundaries among the three arms of government: the executive, legislature and the judiciary, with most of the power in the hands of one person: the President. Governments work so hard to convince the rural masses that there is no difference between the party and government and therefore they are entitled to use government resources for party activities.

Although a few changes have taken place, the words below of American journalist Blaine Harden, concerning African Presidents are as true and strong in many African countries as were when written more than twenty years ago:

> His face is on the money. His photograph hangs in every office in the realm. His ministers wear gold pins with tiny photographs of Him on the lapels of their tailored pinstriped suits. He names streets, football stadiums, hospitals and universities after himself. He carries a silver-inlaid ivory mace or an ornately carved walking stick or a flywhisk or a chiefly symbol. He insists on being called 'doctor' or 'conqueror' or 'teacher' or 'the big elephant' or the 'number one peasant,' or 'the wise old man' or 'the national miracle' or 'the most popular leader in the world.' His every pronouncement is reported on the front page. He sleeps with the wives and daughters of powerful men in government. He shuffles ministers around without warning, paralyzing policy decisions as he undercuts pretenders to the throne. He scapegoats minorities to shore up popular support. He bans all political parties except the one he controls. He rigs elections. He emasculates the courts. He cows the press. He stifles academia. He goes to church . . . He blesses his home region with highways, schools, hospitals, housing projects, irrigation schemes, and a presidential mansion. He packs the civil service with his tribesmen.
>
> He awards uncompetitive, overpriced contracts to foreign companies which grant him, his family, and his associates large kickbacks . . . He is—and makes sure he is known to be the richest man in the country. He buys off rivals by passing out envelopes of cash or import licenses or government land. He questions the patriotism of the few he cannot buy, accusing them of corruption or charging them with 'serving foreign masters.' His enemies are harassed by 'youth wingers' from the ruling party. His enemies are detained or exiled, humiliated or bankrupted; tortured or killed. He uses the resources of the state to feed a cult personality that defines him as incorruptible, all-knowing, physically strong, courageous in battle, sexually potent, and kind to children. His cult equates his personal well being with the well being of the state (Harden, 1990: 217–218).

Dowden (2009: 51) observed that the new presidents in Africa inherited total power from colonial rulers. In addition, the colonial nations had been set up to subjugate, not to serve the citizenry (Harden, 1990: 226). This was worsened by the fact that the states they inherited were made up of old African societies, once self-governing and still held together by their own networks of power and influence. Trying to use the tools of a Western style state to control these rooted societies was like trying to herd cats with a dog training manual. Many of the current successors have not done much to create significant shifts in this regard.

In major decisions affecting the country, animal farm systems will not consult the people. Just as the pigs would go to change the laws at night, animal farm systems manipulate parliaments to pass laws that the masses would not agree with and people are made to believe that they are powerless to do anything about it. Within two years, the Democratic Progressive Party, the ruling party in Malawi, passed eight bills despite vehement opposition and dissatisfaction from the people. They did this based on numerical advantage in parliament. The MPs are under pressure to tow the party line or face reprisals, marginalization or being ruined. Many of them vote against their own consciences (*Malawi News*, June 25–July 1, 2011).

There is a direct relationship between poverty and bad government. Rich countries have good governments; poor countries have bad governments. As citizens learn to hold their governments accountable, their poverty levels go down. A dilemma and paradox that donors have is that they want to help poor countries by giving their money to such governments, governments with very bad governance records. According to Easterly (2007: 132), virtually all poor countries have bad governments, implying that the donors will give their money to bad governments, governments that do not care much about their poor citizens. This is one of the explanations why so much aid given to Africa leaves a lot to be desired in terms of actual reduction in poverty.

Giving more aid without first fixing or panel-beating such governments will not solve the problems of poverty in Africa. And citizens themselves are best placed to fix such governments, otherwise when the attempt to do the fixing seems to come from external drivers or donors, it is all interpreted as "conditionalities" or "interference." The citizenry must do it to create the future they want.

Poor people in Africa cannot honestly expect their governments and even donors to change their lots that much especially when donors sometimes deliberately protect bad governments. Easterly (2007: 137) describes this well when he opines:

> Since donors understandably don't want to admit they are dealing with bad governments, diplomatic language in aid agencies becomes an art form. A war is a 'conflict-related reallocation of resources.' Aid efforts to deal with homicidal warlords are 'difficult partnerships.' Countries whose presidents loot the treasury experience 'governance issues.' Miserable performance is "progress that has not been as fast and comprehensive as envisioned in the PRSP. When government officials want to steal while the aid agency wants development, there are 'differences in priorities and approaches that need to be reconciled.' If debt-relief dollars disappear before reaching the poor, then 'continued progress on the Expenditure Management and Control Program will be needed to maximize the benefits from the HIPC (Heavily Indebted Poor Country) Initiative.'

Concentration of wealth and overstaying in office

The Gabon late President Omar Bongo died in 2009 after ruling Gabon for 42 years. His son, now President, was the Minister of Defense, while his daughter was head of the Presidency and her husband, the Minister of Foreign Affairs. Gabon could only build five kilometers of highway a year, but could find enough money to build a $500 million presidential palace (Mills, 2010: 195). He built Bongo University, Bongo Airport, numerous Bongo Hospitals, Bongo Stadium and Bongo Gymnasium. His home town was renamed Bongoville (Mills, 2010: 196).

Presidents, by their behaviors, set the tone. Franz Fanon summarizes this point well when he says,

> Scandals are numerous, ministers grow rich, their wives doll themselves up, the members of parliament feather their nests and there is not a soul down to the simple policeman or the customs officer who does not join the great procession of corruption. In time, bribery and corruption become a way of life, accepted as a means of getting by, earning a living, obtaining a service or avoiding a hassle (Meredith, 2006: 173).

Much of the collapse of good systems in Africa can be attributed to greed by politicians. Myles Munroe (2009: 19–20) describes the spirit of greed perfectly well when he says,

Greed is the mismanagement of resources for personal benefit, coupled with a disregard for the benefit of others. Greed is when you want more than you need at the expense of everybody else. Greed means I need only one pillow, but I want ten. I need only one little plateful of food at a time, but I want the whole restaurant. Greedy people don't care who gets hurt. They just go after whatever they want and don't concern themselves with other people. They see an opportunity to acquire more money, greater status, or further pleasures, and they charge ahead in pursuit of their selfish goals, regardless how many people they have to trample on in the process.

Leadership in Africa is synonymous with wealth. Politicians are the richest people in Africa. It will be a rare sight indeed to see a poor politician in Africa, not even by African standards. Presidents build unbelievable mansions that do not correlate with their official salaries. Being prosecuted after one's term of office is over is now almost a norm on the continent. It is now almost a norm in Africa and most parts of the world that only the rich or those with rich friends can govern. Democracy is becoming a revolving door for the elite (Ngugi, 2011: 9).

There are too many cases of the likes of Ben Ali, Hosni Mubarak, Frederick Chiluba, Bakili Muluzi and Bingu wa Mutharika. This is one of the reasons why Presidents do not want to leave power after their terms of office expire. It also explains why they want their spouses, brothers or children to take over from them. It also explains why some of them want to die in office. They have skeletons to hide. Presidents who buy private jets costing $30 million while their people are wallowing in poverty are in no hurry to leave the state house.

Greed is the key motivation for Presidents to stay on in power after their terms of office expire. They want to stay on to accumulate more and more wealth and more and more power. They also want to stay on for fear of losing the wealth they have accumulated and fear of possible imprisonment. Stealing government money and stashing it in European banks or buying property in Europe is still fashionable among African leaders.

The greed exemplified by the leaders is the root cause of corruption across the rank and file. The leadership sets the trend. It is very difficult for the system to be corrupted when the leader is clean. And to know whether the leader is clean or not all one has to do is to look at the people. As in the words of Maxwell (2008: 74), "to see how the leader is doing, look at the people."

The extreme opulence of the ruling elite against a background of extreme poverty will increasingly become less accommodated by the poor masses especially with the hard economic and financial times that they are experiencing. Once the masses begin to believe that they could actually be better off minus the current regime, there is almost no stopping them. It was economic issues that tipped the balance in the Arab revolution.

Robert Mugabe has been in power since 1980; Cameroonian President, Paul Biya, has been in power since 1982; Jose Eduardo dos Santos of Angola has been in power since 1979; Yoweri Museveni of Uganda has been in power since 1986. Stepping down in the face of obvious leadership failure is unheard of in Africa. The word "stepping down" does not exist in failed African leaders' lexicology. In fact, in the science of "African leadership," there is no correlation between a leader's tenure of office and his or her performance.

It is not by accident that a period of 10 years (tenure) seems to be a universally agreed cut off point for presidents in most constitutions. If one is destined to make a significant contribution to their country and they cannot do it within 10 years, chances are they will never do it. And if they are a good leader, after 10 years, they should have mentored a team of competent individuals who can ably take over from them and be able to build on their strengths and avoid their mistakes. Those who want to stay for more than 10 years should be honest enough like Emperor Bokasse of Central African Republic to declare that they are kings or emperors and not presidents.

Animal farm systems in Africa love China. They love China because it provides support irrespective of the human rights and governance record of the country concerned. The China Development Bank will invest $10 billion in Zimbabwe's mining and agriculture sector. Given Mr. Mugabe's human rights record this does not help the Zimbabwe governance situation much. Shapiro (2008: 320) observes that China offers authoritarianism combined with Western technology and business methods, and the promise that it can generate faster growth and development than the compromises and delays of democracy. This approach and promise appeal easily to most African governments.

Western governments are cutting down expenditure on supporting governance programs in Africa officially for the reason that it is difficult to justify the expenditure as it is difficult to demonstrate results. One donor officer put it bluntly to me when she said, "We have stopped funding governance programs because African leaders have rejected democracy and opted for authoritarianism, and it is a waste of money to continue forcing them to become what they have rejected." My own suspicion is that pressure and fear of losing influence in Africa for being seen as difficult donors as compared to China, may be forcing Western donors to ease on their democratization and good governance drive. In a meeting, when a donor agency announced that they were dropping their governance program because they were finding it increasingly difficult to demonstrate results, a participant from Zimbabwe raised up his hand and said, "This would be very good news to Mr. Robert Mugabe and he would surely smile at the hearing of it."

These developments justify the need for more efforts in helping take the citizens from the peripheral to the flashpoint as far as governance is concerned.

Culture of fear

Fear is a very important tool for politicians and regimes that want to domesticate their people. Instilling fear in the hearts of the people helps them to continue being in power. This is because they know that once the people lose their fear, the animal farm systems oppressing them will crumble.

In countries where people have not learnt to rise up against animal farm systems, they are paralyzed by fear with a serious corroding effect on self respect and dignity. A culture of fear is one in which people see and know that something is wrong but they do not act. This is more so with people within the system, like a party or organization. Outsiders may actually think that these people are stupid because the anomalies or issues that need challenging are so clear.

A positive development we have observed in the past few years is that there is more space for voicing feelings and dissent in many African countries, especially through the private media. But what is missing is the next step which is mobilization and direct action. This is the difference with Middle East.

While traveling from Malawi to Zimbabwe, I saw a young man in the plane with a carton with about 10 loaves of bread which he bought in Malawi and was taking home to Harare as he could not find a loaf of bread in the whole of Harare. I have seen in Malawi queues of as long as three kilometers of people trying to get fuel at filling stations. Sometimes the fuel is not even there; they are just hoping based on rumors that the fuel will come. People spend nights on the queues waiting for fuel and yet a situation as grave and serious as this does not cause any outrage to move the people into action to hold the people responsible for the situation accountable. Silence and crippling fear have suppressed these people and denied them the simplest services for life in the 21st century. If these people cannot be knocked out of their slumber, expecting real development to happen in their countries would be utter chimera. Growth always comes out of a struggle.

I went to a rural area in Malawi and I was teaching a class of women on leadership. A young woman interrupted me and asked why it was that when she sees "leaders" in her community saying or doing something that she knew was a lie or wrong, she was afraid to stand up and speak her mind. "What was the source of that fear?" she asked me.

Many people in Africa, including highly educated professionals are paralyzed by fear as far as acting on the political situations of their countries is concerned. A culture of fear incapacitates and immobilizes the people. Its primary aim is to instill so much scare so that people should not act let alone express their opinions. If this primary aim fails, the culture aims at creating frustration by letting the people speak as much as they can but the leaders not doing anything about their concerns. This lack of response can eventually convince the people that expressing one's opinion is equally useless, and therefore an option should be to keep quiet.

What the people should understand is that because we are living in the era of information where information can come through backdoor outlets difficult for animal farm systems to monitor, regulate or suppress. Many of such governments will thus adopt the policy of simply closing their ears. Whenever they deem an issue unpalatable, they ignore or shut out from it altogether. However, for anything that is potentially damaging, they are quick to deploy their "Squealers" to come and defend and possibly manipulate the people's perceptions of the same. I remember a minister who was defending a report that his country was experiencing mass starvation. He said it was not true that his country was experiencing mass starvation but the truth was that there was no enough food for many people in the country.

What animal farm systems will not tolerate at any cost and so will do all they can to discourage are free demonstrations. This is because the leaders in animal farm systems usually know that the people are bottled up with so much pain, and demonstrations in such situations have a way of erupting into a revolution. Animal farm systems are demonic systems that survive and thrive on the oppression and suppression of the poor. Some presidents have gone as far as buying beer or alcohol for street vendors as a way of coaxing them not to take part in planned mass demonstrations. Others have a policy of keeping beer prices low with the aim of sedating the young people from developing critique.

A culture of fear assumes an adult-to-child relationship, where the leaders see themselves as adults and so look at the people they are leading as children who need guidance, coercion or intimidation, if necessary. This is why fear is a key tool that animal farm systems use. Animal farm systems instill fear by isolating a few individuals and dealing with them very harshly for the "others to learn from" and so beat themselves to surrender.

Unless the people know that development starts when we conquer fear, animal farm systems will continue to survive and thrive. True freedom and development comes only when the people have conquered their fear. The level of development of a country can be correlated to the degree that the people in the country have conquered their fears, especially the fear of their leaders. This rebalances the nature of the relationship from the adult-to-child one to the desired adult-to-adult one. When people conquer their fear nothing can stop them from any positive change they want. True independence is when one conquers one's fears.

Conclusion

A key characteristic of animal farm systems is that they speak the language of democracy but practice autocracy. In short, the main characteristic of animal farm systems is hypocrisy. When animal farm systems speak, take the exact opposite if you want to understand what it is they are saying, the most probable truth.

A key challenge in standing up against animal farm systems is that in most African countries today, opposition parties are weak, disorganized and divided, making it difficult to create a real challenge and threat to ruling parties. Indeed, many animal farm systems deliberately employ divide-and-rule strategies to sow impotence and remove the sting in the opposition. The opposition party themselves cannot be relied upon to fight ruling parties exhibiting animal farm characteristics, as inherently and probably, they are animal farm systems themselves.

The most prevalent and common sign of animal farm systems is poor governance which eventually and inevitably results in poor economic performance. Sustainability equals good governance. Any prosperity that lacks the foundation of good governance is not sustainable. Good governance creates the preconditions and the enabling environment in which prosperity can thrive. It is not by coincidence that countries with good governance records are more prosperous than those that do not have.

Breaking animal farm systems involves preventing abuse of power by finding collective ways to keep leaders committed to their visions and plans, institutionalizing meritocracy, ensuring transparency and accountability to the citizens, encouraging group and team recognition and deliberately reducing individual visibility and brilliance to neutralize the culture of personality cult, distributing power and wealth fairly and exorcising fear among the poor masses.

CHAPTER 6: WHY LEADERSHIP FAILS IN AFRICA AND WHAT AFRICANS CAN DO ABOUT IT

Introduction

If we called out for all books written so far on the subject of "leadership," we would hardly have shelves to accommodate them all together—there are just so many researchers and writers who have written extensively on the subject over the ages of history. For this reason, writing on leadership isn't as easy, for what new thing can one write about it? What is interesting perhaps is how little practice is drawn out of these volumes on the subject especially on the African continent, or maybe there is something terribly wrong with the type of knowledge being promoted as leadership knowledge here?

It is my opinion that if Mr. Barack Obama was living in Kenya, chances are very high that he would not have become the President of Kenya because the system may not have allowed him to do so. It took me twelve years after I had begun speaking in international conferences to finally get an invitation to speak at a conference in my own home country. I had to be validated outside before I could be trusted inside. Behind these two examples lies a major explanation of the African leadership problem: almost impregnable systems that allow old and mostly bad leaders to flourish and at the same time constrain or limit the space for new leaders with new ideas. It must be emphasized again that leadership, especially in Africa, is not for "chickens" or for men and women without backbones. The cost of effective leadership is too high for many people. But people usually don't take these considerations before committing to undertake leadership responsibilities.

Building on the previous chapters, in this chapter, I will discuss my understanding of leadership, what I believe to be the main demons afflicting African leadership; and some suggestions to addressing the same.

Understanding Leadership in Africa

If you want to understand the stage of leadership development in a country, first observe how political parties are run and how election campaigns are managed, and second look at a country's national curriculum, how practical it is in addressing questions of leadership.

I believe that there is a very close correlation between a country's maturity of democracy and its leadership development. Because political parties are the most visible organizations and they represent the dominant model of leadership in a country, the way they are run and how election campaigns in general are conducted will have a lot to say about the country's leadership ideals.

As for the national curriculum, effective educational systems aim at developing independent minds—individuals who can question anything and everyone not only with words but also with action. In most African countries, curricula have been "politicized" with the aim of taming whole populations. *When people are ignorant, evil politicians smile.*

I was invited to talk about African leadership at a meeting in the Netherlands. I asked myself what African leadership is. Does such a thing exist?

Can Africa claim political, economic, technological or cultural leadership? The answer is obviously no. We are hearing that the centre of religion, especially Christianity, has shifted to Africa, but is such a development contributing consciously to enhancing good leadership on the continent? At a strategic level, we are yet to see such a conscious contribution. In a continent of close to one billion people out of a global population of seven billion, Africa (minus South Africa) today contributes only one percent of the total global trade (economy) from about five percent in the 1970s.

If one wants to understand leadership in Africa, simply by looking at how political parties are run and the ability of the curricula to develop ability for critique in practical terms, they will conclude that African leadership does not exist or it is still in infancy.

The standard for measuring leadership effectiveness all over the world revolves around four main areas: vision, inspiration, integrity and influence. It is also around these areas that leadership challenges can be understood at a strategic level. Vision means defining what the future should look like or the future we aspire, while inspiration means motivating, energizing and aligning people towards the defined desired future. It is vision and inspiration that distinguish true leadership.

It is important to point out that being visionary does not mean living in the future or idly day-dreaming how wonderful it will feel when the vision has been achieved. A true or visionary leader lives in the present but his or her decisions and actions are determined by and are tuned to his or her vision or the future he or she aspires.

African Leadership Challenges

Against this background, I will present what I believe to be the five key African leadership challenges which if addressed would lift the continent and its organizations to compete favorably in the 21st Century global economy to the benefit of the poor masses. These key challenges are: inadequate long term thinking (low visioning power) and lack of effective succession plans because of selfishness and greed; inadequate motivation among followers because their role is downplayed in defining and ensuring effective leadership and also because there is disconnection of leaders from realty; low integrity of those holding leadership positions; inability to exercise positive influence by those holding leadership positions; and finally over concentration of power in politics as compared to other sources of power in a normal society: business, civil society, religion and centers of higher learning (academia).

Inadequate visioning and inspiring power

According to Peter Drucker, "leadership is lifting a person's vision to higher sights, the raising of a person's performance to higher standard, the building of personality beyond its normal limitations." We can therefore say that leadership is lifting the citizens' vision to higher sights, the raising of organizational mobilization performance to higher standard and the building of their mobilization and organization beyond its normal limitations.

If leadership is about vision and inspiration, many leaders and political parties simply do not have these. Many leaders have actually stopped pretending to be visionary anymore, but vision and inspiration are the real driving force of any organizational success. According to Burt Nanus, there is no more powerful engine driving an organization forward towards excellence and long range success than an attractive, worthwhile, achievable vision for the future, widely shared. A truly powerful vision becomes an inspiration and a strong magnet pulling the organizational effort into its desired future. Many organizations today have the challenge of having too many brilliant and efficient technocrats and too few far sighted visionaries. Leaders focus on creating tomorrow rather than maintaining today or defending yesterday. In the absence of a transcending and shared vision personalities will always prevail over the bigger collective good entrenching the personality cult syndrome.

The big questions today are: Are our visions magnetic enough to pull our organizations and our people to our collectively desired futures? Are the futures defined collectively? Is our leadership inspiring enough to keep citizens fully engaged in their struggle for full citizenship?

Related to inadequate long term thinking is the issue of non-existent or ineffective succession plans.

Succession planning

The great leader who leaves behind a crumbling empire is no great at all. A leader who is not concerned about leaving behind a stronger and better foundation for the next leaders is not a real leader. A leader who fires all the intelligent people and surrounds himself or herself with sycophants or yes-people is not a real leader. A leader who is afraid of intelligent and critical followers is not a mature leader. A true leader should be able to mentor and coach at least five people within the organization that should be able to lead better than himself or herself because they have learnt from both his and her strengths and weaknesses.

A true leader is ready and prepared for any eventuality. A true leader can be defeated by never surprised. He or she recognizes and respects his or her own dispensability and mortality. He is not under the usual illusion that "death always happens to the other guy because I have never died before but I have seen a lot of people dying." Because he or she puts the organization first before his or her interest, he or she takes great effort to ensure the sustainability of the organization long after he or she is gone through effective succession planning mechanisms.

We should also add that he or she does not impose their spouse, brother, son or daughter as their successor unless it is a family business and even if it is a family business, a wise leader will do so if the relative is the most qualified to take that responsibility.

Inadequate motivation or broken leadership contracts

No adult can follow anybody for long without any clear motive and having that motive fulfilled. It is the understanding and fulfilling of these motives that constitute leadership contracts. There are three key leadership contracts: wealth or riches; security and; expression of one's values about an ideal world. In wealth or riches, the leadership contract says, "If you follow me, I will give you money or I will make you rich." This is the primary promise of the private sector.

In security, the leadership contract says, "If you follow me, I will give you job security for the rest of your life." This is the promise of the civil service. Finally, the values contract says, "If you follow me, I will help you change the world and shape it according to your values. I will help you fight poverty and injustice." This is the promise of NGOs and civil society organizations.

In many organizations, members of staff are not clear what they are being promised; their motives are not fulfilled, making frustration (and frustration is always a result of unfulfilled motives or expectations) the number one problem in most organizations the world over. The same applies to citizens. Politicians come with wonderful promises upon which trust is established but soon after, the politicians abandon their promises and run away from their people.

Broken contracts are also related to lack of integrity where integrity is understood as matching of one's words and one's actions. The people have come to generally expect their leaders to default on their words. They have come to accept not to take their leaders seriously. This has come to shape individual's motives negatively. In an atmosphere of mistrust between leaders and followers it is self-serving interests that prevail.

Leadership and followers

There are two reasons that explain why Africa is poor: bad leaders and weak followers. Much has been written about bad leaders but very little about the weak followers who also happen to comprise the majority of victims of leadership abuse and the underdevelopment commonplace on the African continent.

While not explicit, in most leadership definitions, the meaning of leadership has consciously or unconsciously evolved to mean "leaders." Today, when we talk about leadership we are almost automatically talking about individuals we call leaders; leadership is equated to leaders.

In a recent training course, I asked the participants what leadership is. Their general agreement was that "leadership is what leaders do." This seems to be the universally accepted understanding of leadership especially in Africa.

Robert Kelly observes that in searching so zealously for better leaders we tend to lose sight of the people those leaders will lead. Without his armies, Napoleon Bonaparte was just a man with grandiose ambitions (who could not even conquer a village). Organizations stand or fall partly on the basis of how well their leaders lead and partly on the basis of how well the followers follow. In short, leadership = leaders + followers; and effective leadership = effective leaders + effective followers. The "dance" between leaders and followers is what determines leadership effectiveness. In conventional thinking of leadership, the role of followers has been greatly downplayed. Success in organizations is attributed to many things including opportunities, the economy, timing, chemistry, luck and of course, effective leaders. All these are true but the one thing that all successful organizations have is empowered and engaged followership.

Empowered followers will help leaders become better leaders while disempowered followers will inevitably create dictators. It is my personal conviction that overall leadership effectiveness has to do more with effective followers than effective leaders because the true signs of outstanding leadership are found among the followers. In most organizations we seem to have adopted an "adult-to-child" model of leadership where leaders are seen as parents and followers are seen as children to always be told what to do, a bunch of people not to be taken seriously.

Recognizing and putting in its right place the role of followers in defining effective leadership is a major if not the most difficult challenge at community, organizational and national levels in Africa. In improving leadership effectiveness, followers have failed more than leaders. It is ineffective followers who create ineffective leaders and dictators. In relative terms, leadership development efforts will need to focus more on followers than leaders. How much power or influence in shaping the leadership agenda do citizens have in African countries?

Disconnection of leaders from reality

When leaders monopolize leadership they soon become disconnected from reality. Many times reality is with the followers. Followers have a better perspective of what ought to be done while many times leaders are driven more by what they want to do rather than what ought to be done for the high and common good. It is important to recognize that leaders are not necessarily more intelligent or smarter than the followers. Being a leader can be intoxicating, giving one the illusion of omnipotence and omniscience—the feeling that "because I am a leader, I am more powerful and more intelligent than my followers therefore I don't need to listen to them." Robert Kelly observed, "Followership is not a person but a role, and what distinguishes followers from leaders is not intelligence or character but the roles they play . . . effective followers and effective leaders are often the same people playing different parts at different parts of the day."

When I am practicing as a leadership development practitioner and writer, I am being a leader. When I go to church, my pastor is the leader and I am a follower but I am the same person. In order to improve the overall leadership effectiveness of my practice and my church I need to be equally effective as a leader and as a follower. I need to give my best as a leadership development practitioner, and I must also help my church demonstrate the same things I teach others. I must take a questioning stance where these are not being demonstrated.

A key leadership success factor for leaders is to listen to followers and to identify with them and their aspirations. In short, it is humility. Because they have stopped truly listening, many leaders have lost their legitimacy and relevance and their leadership is not truly sustainable.

Shunning listening to followers is the beginning of the death of leadership. When leaders stop listening they become increasingly irrelevant and therefore ineffective. The ability to receive constructive feedback, especially critical feedback, and use that feedback for further leadership self-development is a key sign of maturity for leaders. Unfortunately, this is very rare, incredibly so, in Africa. Most organizations, like political parties in Africa have succeeded in teaching their followers to shut up, follow orders and cover up mistakes, the number one reason why other continents are outpacing us, leaving us behind by light years. We have examples of followers who have been punished, fired, imprisoned or even killed for giving constructive feedback to leaders. Talking on leadership, Harry Truman, one of the most respected Presidents of the US once remarked, "The President hears a hundred voices telling him that he is the greatest man in the world. He must listen carefully indeed to hear the one voice that tells him that he is not."

Lack of integrity

I have always wondered whether there is anything fundamentally wrong with the African character. Is it true that Africans have no capacity for high levels of integrity and ethics? To put it bluntly, is it true that Africans are cursed with a natural lack of leadership capacity? Although not true, unfortunately, observed evidence seem to support these notions. Good African leadership seems to be the exception rather than the norm. Of the prominent leaders on the continent we would be lucky to identify really good and effective leaders beyond the fingers of one hand. But just as we do not judge a religion by the behavior of its people, it would also be wrong to judge African leadership by its individual leaders though admittedly this is a difficult concept to understand. Not all people who profess to be Christians or Muslims are so in their hearts. Similarly, not all individuals who hold leadership positions are leaders in their hearts. Many leaders at the helm today were not voted into power in the true sense of the word; they had rigged the elections and had put themselves into power, without true legitimacy. Initially, some were good and the people had indeed put their trust in them but power and greed had corrupted them and they threw away their developmental agendas and embraced "self-enrichment" as their sole purpose for exercising "leadership." Many fall in this category and we can point them out even in the dark.

The integrity challenge in Africa can be traced to the setting that builds us in terms of social organization: the village in which our culture is based on five main principles:

- Sharing and collective ownership of opportunities, responsibilities and challenges
- The importance of people and relationships over things
- Participatory decision making and leadership
- Loyalty to the clan; and
- Reconciliation as a goal for conflict management

These principles were practiced at a village or clan level and generally, unlike other groups like the Jews, we have not been able to transfer them effectively into the modern urban-based life. The result is shadows arising from the same that have come to characterize "African leadership" including nepotism, tribalism, a suppression of meritocracy, inability to give or accept constructive feedback and inability to correct things when they go wrong. Good leaders get under pressure to support whole villages, to support funerals and weddings which are usually beyond their means. Many succumb to these pressures and become corrupted.

Over-concentration of power in politics

In Africa, there are very few economic spoils available outside politics; politics is the most popular route to wealth in Africa. The other centers of power in society: business, civil society, centers of higher learning and religion are not as lucrative as politics. This is why everyone: doctors, lawyers, teachers, preachers, literally everyone, wants to become a member of parliament (MP). And there is cutthroat competition to become an MP. In America or in Europe, if one loses the contest for the house of parliament or president, they go back to exercise power in the other centers of power: institutions of higher learning, civil society, business and may be religion. In Africa, one goes back to poverty, bankruptcy, imprisonment or death. This over-concentration of power has turned politics, which is the epitome of leadership in Africa, into a lucrative business. And we all know that the purpose of business is to make a profit; serving people is secondary.

Implications of the challenges

With low visioning power and lack of sense of direction and priorities the people spend more time complaining about present problems rather than building the future they want. People cannot complain and build at the same time. Inadequate motivation leads to reduced loyalty. When leaders lack integrity people don't take them seriously. This leads to institutionalized corruption. The leaders set the tone by their integrity or by lack of it. A former Minister of Information in Mobutu Sese Seko's government once said whenever Mobutu sent his boys to "collect" say, one million dollars from the accountant, the boys would ask for two million, and the request to the central bank would even be a higher figure. In the end, the actual money released would be almost five million, the four million being for those in between and so unaccounted for. Leaders do set the tone by their integrity or by their lack of it. *What you do speaks so loud; I can't hear what you say.*

Organizational systems

The combined implications of the above leadership challenges are the creation and nurturing or cultivation of negative organizational systems. Organizational systems, whether bad or good, are more powerful than individuals because groups are holier or more evil than individuals. Changing faces or individuals in positions of leadership does not necessarily mean changing systems. I heard a woman from Tunisia on TV saying, "We have chased away Ben Ali (the then President) but his system is still here." Another one said of Egypt, "We have chased away President Hosni Mubarak but the real Mubarak is still very strong in our minds." A news reader on TV in Malawi mistakenly referred to Hastings Kamuzu Banda as the President of the country twelve years after Banda's death. That showed how deeply Banda had gone into his and many Malawians' subconscious mind.

An old man challenged me when I was facilitating a vision crafting exercise in a rural village. He said, "Young man, I was here when the colonialists were ruling this country. I was also here when the first African President took over from them and also when the next President took over from him. I am still here with the current President. They all said they will bring development but this village is just as poor if not worse than it was in the colonial times. On what basis are you saying that this exercise will develop us?" At that point, I realized that the country had changed faces in the Presidential palace but had not changed the system.

When a President becomes unpopular, his members of parliament and ministers will simply defect to the next individual's party with their attitudes, values and behaviors intact. They are often received in the new party without any scrutiny because the (new) party they join represent the same system they are coming from.

A system is a mould that produces the attitudes, values and behaviors of a group of people. Systems create the people's expectations and responses to decisions and actions taken by leadership. Systems may be liberating or domesticating, empowering or disempowering, optimistic or fatalistic; and people-centered or self-centered. It is the domesticating, disempowering, fatalistic and self-centered systems that I refer to as animal farm systems in this discussion.

Systems are more powerful and sustainable than individuals. It can be argued that Mr. Barack Obama could not have become the President of America if he had decided to form his own party rather than join the Democratic Party. The Democratic Party is a system. The death of Osama bin Laden did not mean the death of the terrorist system or his group Al-Qaeda. It can also be argued that the African National Congress (ANC) wins elections in South Africa more on the strength of the party than its candidates because it is a strong system.

Countries with better systems are stronger than those with more powerful individuals. Systems sustain themselves while individuals cannot. A metaphor of a system that comes to mind is a watchtower in a battlefield where the soldiers with the machine gun on the tower has a very long queue of soldiers behind him or her waiting to step in once he or she is shot or killed.

A system is a mould that produces predictable results unless the mould itself is changed. A system shapes values, attitudes and behaviors. When the attitudes, values and behaviors between the individual and the system differ, a conflict between the individual and the system ensues. If the individual is weak, the system will expel him or her. If the individual is stronger he or she will change the system for good or for worse. People like Harold Camping, an American evangelist, can cheat the whole world by declaring that the world would end on 21st May, 2011 but their systems are not strong enough to force them to apologize and step down.

Effective leaders change their systems for the better while bad leaders change their systems for the worse.

Systems determine which values will prevail or be practiced in the organization. Individual values don't matter much in a system. An example is a good individual who joins a parliament full of opportunists. He ends up frustrated in trying to change it. Worse still he or she ends up being converted or "hedge-clipped" just for the sake of her "sanity and peace." One of Russia's Presidents was holding a public rally. In the audience, one whispered, "He's saying so many good things and he is even criticizing his predecessor. He is a hypocrite; why did he not criticize the former President when he was his minister?" The President overheard him. In a seemingly angry voice he shouted, "Who said that?" The person kept quiet. The President smiled and said, "For the same reason you are hiding I did not criticize the former President when I was his minister." In short, he was saying "the system at that time did not allow me to express my views." Going against the system can be very dangerous.

A simplest example of a system is the case of a woman whose husband went to South Africa from Zambia to look for a job when she was pregnant. He promised to come back and pick her when he found the job and was settled. When he arrived in South Africa, he wrote his wife telling her he had found the job and he would come back as soon as he got settled. The man never came back. Years later, the child, now a big boy, asked his mother who his father was and where he was. The mother narrated the story to him.

At 21, he told his mother he wanted to travel to South Africa to look for his father and bring him back home for her. He bade his mother farewell and left. A few days after arriving in South Africa, he wrote her mother that he had found his father and they together would be coming back soon. He too, like his father, never came back and she never heard from him again. The mother lost both the husband and the son to the "South African system." A system is a mould that produces results. Unless it is changed it will produce the same shape of results.

Bad systems make good people within the system fail to exercise good leadership. Bad systems shrink the space for good to prevail. They enable bad leaders to emerge and flourish and good ones to falter. Good systems enable good people to exercise good leadership. Good systems make it hard for bad leaders to exercise bad leadership. Good systems enable good leaders to flourish and bad ones to falter. If you took the devil to heaven he would feel so uncomfortable he would run away.

Empowering systems are relevant; they connect with universal human values and are sustainable. Animal farm systems are irrelevant, not connected to people's universal values and will eventually disintegrate no matter how strong they may look on the surface. Every animal farm system has a seed for self-poisoning and eventual self-destruction. If this was not so, the world would have ended a long time ago or evil systems like the Nazis would still be around in their original form.

Many people and organizations are unconscious victims of the systems they inherit. Negative systems are difficult to run; they sap a lot of energy from the people, maintaining them because, as in the words of Mandela, "the freedom flame cannot be smothered by evil men." Evil people have to spend a lot of energy to smother the good in the people they lead, especially in these days of higher levels of political consciousness. Most importantly, negative systems serve only a few individuals at the expense of many. The energy spent in defending and maintaining negative systems could be better invested in cultivating vision, inspiration, integrity and influence or simply positive systems and benefits more people.

Many organizations and countries in Africa are going in circles because they are preoccupied with changing faces of people or leaders in office rather than changing systems. This is dealing with symptoms rather than root causes.

Animal farm systems embrace the body of democracy just to "fit in" but they reject the spirit of democracy through their attitudes, values and behaviors. They will build structures, policies and institutions of democracy but these will be devoid of the attitudes, values and behaviors of genuine democracy. In short, animal farm systems will master the language of democracy but refuse to walk their talk.

A key distinguishing mark of animal farm systems is the *if you do not agree with my point of view, then you are my enemy and therefore we should not co-exist* syndrome which creates fear. Animal farm systems are not sustainable in the long term for the very reason that anything that is built on fear in not sustainable. We know people who have been fired, jailed, exiled or even killed for holding different points of view. Hypocrisy is a key distinguishing mark of animal farm systems. They exist primarily to serve the selfish interests of their leaders, key of which are money and power. Many leaders in Africa have not learnt from Napoleon Bonaparte's great regret, "Had my council properly advised me, had they opposed me at times, France would have ruled supreme" (Grant, 2009: 348). *If there are no quarrels in a group, the people are not being truthful and honest with each other.*

Many development initiatives fail because most of them fail to articulate clearly how they will deal with the attitudes, values and behaviors in the systems they are working with. In *the POST* of Thursday, May 12, 2011 in an article entitled "World Bank Launches a 10-Year Strategy for Africa" the World Bank Representative in Zambia announced that the new strategy would focus on faster economic growth, creating more jobs, reducing poverty and increasing women land rights. The Bank would also improve higher education, reduce corruption, service delivery and increase protection against climate change. These will be implemented under the three pillars of: competitiveness and employment, vulnerability and resilience; and governance and public sector capacity.

Unless this strategy is implemented by empowering systems, it is likely to fail since animal farm systems will continue to produce similar results unless the systems themselves are changed. Unless the social accountability efforts planned under the governance pillar effectively manage to transform animal farm systems to empowering ones through fundamental changes at the attitude, values and behavior levels, the Bank will continue to grapple with high levels of corruption and theft which are constraining its efforts now. Corruption and theft are inevitable results of animal farm systems.

The fight against animal farm systems in Africa is essentially the fight against sanctioned corruption. In many countries corruption has become the system in which the powerful exploit the less powerful who in turn exploit the powerless (Harden, 1990: 45). Pronouncements by governments that they are fighting corruption have become a great tickling joke, a source of derision. The World Bank estimates that 40 percent of the money it gives out to third world countries in grants and loans is stolen by leaders.

Cultivating empowering organizational systems

Without effective systems, no human progress is possible at any level from individual, community, national, continental or global. The challenge of real leadership in Africa involves instituting and cultivating empowering systems. It also involves challenging, destroying and replacing bad systems with good ones. Leadership development efforts for individuals and groups must be aimed at encouraging them to recognize and challenge negative systems without fear. People must be encouraged to question decisions and actions taken by leaders without fear of reprisal or punishment. Leadership and human resources management schools, especially in Africa, must adjust their curricula to rise up to this challenge.

An example of an empowering system is given by Nelson Mandela in his book, *Conversations with Myself* (2010:344):

> At meetings of the African National Congress (ANC) I often stressed that I did not want weak comrades or puppets who would swallow anything I said simply because I was President of the organization. I called for a healthy relationship in which we could address issues, not as a master and servants, but as equals in which each comrade would express his or her views freely and frankly and without fear of victimization or marginalization.

Contrary to the above, recently I heard an African President, at a public rally, addressing his cabinet ministers and MPs: "This is my party. I started it myself. If you are not happy, you are free to leave. And I can assure you the party will go on and you will not be missed." None of the ministers or MPs protested. In fact, they forced a smile each. "Are there no men or women in that party who can stand up against that demeaning treatment?" one may ask. There are, but the system has reduced them to mere powerless boys and girls.

A classic example of how an empowering system should work is a scene in the film, "Mandela and de Klerk." In this particular scene, in a cabinet meeting a junior minister raises his hand and asks President Botha to step down in a vote of no confidence. Visibly surprised and shocked the President asks who else is in agreement with the minister. Several hands go up. That settles it. The President is fired (of course after expressing some anger and disappointment at the "ungrateful ministers" as he called them). This is an example of a system that gives space to good people to express views without fear and those views are respected. This is a system that allows the power of good to overshadow the power of evil.

In how many of our political parties or organizations can leaders step down when they fail to deliver on their promises? Can leaders be fired by their followers?

I went to an office to ask for an individual who I knew was the founder of the organization. "He was fired," the receptionist told me. "How so, he was the founder of this organization?" I asked in surprise. "He was, yes, but he did something wrong and he was fired. In America even founders are fired because individuals do not own public organizations even if they are founders," she told me. In many parts of Africa, this is just inconceivable. Here, many public organizations are run as private property.

Africa's greatest leadership disease is the suppression of dissent and opinions that leaders don't like and discouragement of developmental or constructive arguments on issues to reach consensus. The "if you don't agree with me you are my enemy" syndrome coupled with fear of bright and independent minded people are key leadership vices. A leader of an African country was willing to sacrifice about 50 percent of his government's budgetary support from a donor country by deporting the high commissioner of that country because the high commissioner had pointed out the President's failures in observing good governance. What really surprised me was that the President was 80 years old and all along we have been taught in Africa that elderly people are custodians of wisdom.

Dismantling Africa's colonial educational system

To illustrate the power of systems, my friend, Monica Kapiriri (2011) talks about the "colonial African educational mould" which was designed by the colonial masters to make sure the African educational system primarily serves the interests of Europe. It was inherited by the African founding fathers and passed on to the current leaders. This system is still manifested in African countries curricula today. Since the mould was meant to serve colonial interests, this explains why most curricula on the continent are largely irrelevant to the real needs of the countries and to the African 21st century African situation.

To break this system, Monica advises that we need to go back to the drawing board and dismantle the mould and replace it with one that can developmentally shift the continent. This will help us to demonstrate that we have moved from a feeling that we are inferior; to celebrating Africa's uniqueness; and using this uniqueness to our advantage in our communities and in defining our place in the world. Monica also encourages teaching and learning by example. If agriculture professors have personal model farms, for example, their students will follow. We must move beyond accumulating certificates and degrees as souvenirs to translating them into real value not only in our personal but also community lives. The key question is: How are our bachelors, doctorates and post doctorate degrees benefiting our villages?

Monica concludes by challenging us that "as it was in the colonial times, so it is today and will surely continue to be unless the colonial mould is broken."

We need leaders in the important fields of life. Any child on the continent can mention three top most celebrities without any struggle but African graduates will struggle to mention the names of three topmost African scientists if they can. This is because we have agreed that music and film celebrities are more important than scientists, an attitude that needs to be changed.

Creating empowering organizational systems

Developing leadership effectiveness in organizations requires energy, effort and work by both the leaders and followers. Peter Drucker advises that the only things that evolve by themselves in an organization are disorder, friction and malperformance. Addressing the challenges discussed above can be summarized under five broad headings: need for organizational DNA; raising consciousness of the culture of the organization; replacing disempowering systems with empowering ones; a need to improve mutual accountability; and encouraging individuals to create personal "go to hell funds."

Organizational DNA

To ensure an effective and inspiring vision there is a need to move beyond survival instincts. We have to propel towards concerns about defining an organization's unique contribution in the world, and creating the legacy we want to leave behind. We have to reflect, honestly, on whether if we stopped existing, we would be truly missed. This is done by creating a compelling, bold, ambitious, vivid, inspiring, transforming, concise, bright and brilliant ideal picture of the organization—a desired picture of the organization some years into the future. When fully internalized by both leaders and followers, it is this ideal picture that becomes the magnet, pulling the organization into its desired future; it is this picture internalized by the leaders and the followers that becomes the DNA of the organization.

Find below an example of an ideal picture:

> The year 2015. NGO X is the number one Child-Centered Community Development Organization in Africa. It is the organization of choice for staff and among stakeholders seeking synergistic collaboration.
>
> It is agile, flexible, innovative, adaptive and resilient. It is capable of efficiently and effectively empowering communities through enhancing active participation in their own development.
> It has put in place mechanisms for accountability, transparency and visibility. NGO X is working closely with government and other key stakeholders.

Mutual accountability

Once the "magnet" has been established, the leaders and followers must go to work in turning it into reality. This means aligning all aspects of the organization to its desired future. At this point, mutual accountability becomes the most important success factor. The leaders and followers will need to agree on mutual accountability mechanisms. The leaders will need to develop a list of their expectations from the followers and the followers will develop their list of expectations from the leaders.

It may be something like: In order to turn our organizational ideal picture into reality, we, as followers (staff) expect our leaders to:

- Be more open to critical feedback
- Listen to us more and to demonstrate that our ideas are taken seriously
- Be more transparent in all critical information that we need
- Recognize our contribution more
- Involve us more in decision making
- Share benefits more equitably
- Recognize and respect the need for work-life balance
- Interfere less

In order to turn our organizational ideal picture into reality, we, as leaders (managers) expect our staff to:

- Demonstrate conscious internalization of the organizational ideal picture
- See the big picture beyond their own jobs and departments
- Demonstrate more understanding of "organizational realities"
- Embrace, rather than resist change implied by the ideal picture
- Be more proactive in making improvement suggestions
- Demonstrate more maturity in giving us feedback
- Demonstrate more team work in their efforts
- Demonstrate more loyalty to the organization

These will need to be negotiated until an agreement is reached and then a monitoring mechanism will be put in place on the frequency for giving each other (leaders and followers) feedback and reward and punishments for performance or non-performance. Similarly important is the continuous communication of the ideal picture by the leaders. The ideal picture cannot be communicated enough.

Raising consciousness of the culture of the organization

Introduce and nurture a positive and empowering organizational culture by reflecting and acting on the following strategic questions:

- What is valued in this organization—people or things/ loyalty or performance etc.?
- What is rewarded in this organization—lies or truth?
- Who are the heroes or villains in this organization—real men or women on one hand or sycophants?
- Where does our organization allocate most of its resources—defending the past or creating the future we want (our ideal picture)?
- Who is valued more in recruitment for higher positions—insiders or outsiders?

What does this analysis tell us about our organizational alignment to the ideal picture? What changes do we need to make so that we can become more aligned?

Replace disempowering systems with more empowering ones

Changing established disempowering systems is difficult and hard work. But there are opportune times when organizations and their systems are more vulnerable and acceptant to change. These offer the window of opportunity for change. Times of leadership change—before new leaders are settled are times of opportunities. At these moments, the leaders are more pliable because many times they are not yet corrupted by the system. We must hit the iron while it is still hot. These would be ideal moments for instituting the ideal picture and its accountability system. Once this is done, the whole organization, especially the followers must be vigilant against any first signs of "undemocratic tendencies." *A lion which kills a bad man but is not killed instead will soon kill a good man.* Times of leadership change are also ideal for review of organizational policies and culture, to make sure negative elements are removed and positive ones bolstered, that all loopholes are tightened.

Leaders do not become dictators overnight; the process is gradual, but when not checked they eventually grow into full-length dictators. Dictatorship grows through phases and if not stopped in time, it reaches a critical point, a kind of threshold beyond which it becomes a full grown monster in a corrupt, almost irreparable system. The people of Zimbabwe, for example, may have to wait until Mr. Mugabe is dead. This was the same challenge the people of Libya were facing.

Replacing bad systems with good ones also involves checking what flows through the systems and the motives of the sources of such flows. The flows can include information or misinformation, fear or courage. The first point is to objectively check the effect the flows have on the people in the organization and whether this is what we would want to see, and most importantly, whether this is moving us in the direction of the future we aspire to attain.

A "go to hell fund"

Bad systems prevail in organizations when individuals are financially disempowered and totally dependent on the organization. Poor people are easy to manipulate because they are dominated by fear of losing their jobs if they go against the system. Poverty is one of the key tools corrupt and bad systems use to perpetuate their grip to power and system. *Poverty is the mother of all crimes.* A casual look will indicate that there is a very high correlation between high levels of democracy and riches in rich countries on one hand and high levels of autocracy and fear in poor countries. This means two things: organizations that embrace democracy or empowering systems are more likely to prosper than those that do not. It also means that when people are financially independent, they are more likely to challenge negative and disempowering systems. The implications for human resources management is to encourage individuals and advocate for policies that enable staff to create their own "go to hell funds"—an amount of money in one's account that can enable them to live at the same standard of life if they happen to be out of work for a whole year. This amount of money emboldens one to "speak their true mind on issues" and to "conquer fear."

Conclusion

If you ask anyone today, even those you consider to be epitome of bad leadership, who their leadership role models are, they will not give names of Idi Amin Dada, Bokasse, Abacha, Mobutu or Pol Pot. They will likely mention Mandela, Ketumire Masire, Mahatma Gandhi, Mother Teresa and Martin Luther King. Lack of knowledge of leadership is not the challenge. The challenge today isn't whether we know so much about leadership or not; the challenge today is to move our level of practice to our level of knowledge.

The real work of both leaders and followers is first of all, to surface and confront contradictions in themselves and then encourage the organization to consciously do the same: to also surface and confront contradictions in their organizational systems. This is an integrity issue—encouraging and challenging individuals and organizations to practice what they preach. Remember, *if you really want to go to Mount Olympus, make sure every step you make takes you nearer there.* This will allow good and empowering systems to flourish and bad and disempowering systems to starve to death. Individuals must be encouraged to recognize and challenge wrong systems without fear.

What Africa needs is not billions of dollars in aid but good and responsible leadership. More money without good leadership first only encourages more corruption in those in power. What Africa needs is a revolution of values and systems, from disempowering systems to empowering systems.

The continent, countries, communities and organizations are all interrelated as a grand system, and change—positive change—can begin at any of these levels. The challenge is: Can we be pioneers in instituting and cultivating empowering systems in our organizations, systems which can in turn act as catalysts for positive change on the continent, change that everyone in the world is looking forward to, a change that will make Africa useful to the world, not as it is, a perpetual burden to civilization?

CHAPTER 7: BREAKING ANIMAL FARM SYSTEMS

Introduction

Poor people should not be seen as utterly helpless, at the mercy of others, civil society organizations mostly, to lift them out of poverty, a view most publications and groups would like to promote. Poor people should be seen as a product of their decisions and actions and should always be encouraged to think thus. A primary way they can do this is to question and challenge the decisions and actions by others that are not in their interest.

Inadequate development and expression of critique among the poor is a defining element, the key constraint to development in Africa. Poor people must be able to identify and challenge negative and manipulative systems; they must be knocked out of slumber for them to realize that it is possible in this life to free themselves of the shackles fetters of the oppressors and exploiters. At a time Western donors, with their emphasis on good governance, are losing their influence in Africa because of the ascendance of China which does not "interfere in local governance issues," the need for poor people to mobilize against animal farm systems cannot be overemphasized.

Breaking animal farm systems

Animal farm systems thrive by maintaining and entrenching the status quo among the people. The hope for Africa is in breaking the animal farm systems and replacing them with empowering systems—systems that are conscious and capable of self correction.

If we understand development as "the awakening of consciousness," animal farm systems can be broken through raising of consciousness among the people. This can be done by, first of all, facilitating processes for the people to draw ideal and aspirational pictures of the future they desire on one hand and the undesired current picture on the other. Associating maximum pleasure with the ideal picture and maximum pain with the present is the way of enhancing political and developmental consciousness. This is why Moses, in his message to the Israelites in bondage in Egypt, told them he would take them from the hell of the bondage in Egypt to a heaven, a land flowing with milk and honey in Canaan.

Exposure through the Internet and television on how better their peers are in the West will continue to make it more difficult for governments in developing countries to satisfy the youths. This, coupled with the live broadcasts of revolutions in other parts of the world like the Arab world, for example, would give them an idea of what is possible. With tighter immigration controls to the US, Europe and even South Africa, it means that the pressure of dissatisfaction will be contained within the countries, creating potential for a time bomb therein. Too many unemployed and idle young people are a potential revolutionary force. However, many young people in Africa, including University graduates, do not have a full and conscious grasp and comprehension of the African governance problem and its implications on development and indeed their own lives and those of generations to come. They may have an intellectual agreement but have mostly not moved to emotional involvement which is the true demonstration of conviction. Most of them have not been involved at all in and with the issue. Awakening their consciousness is the need of the hour.

The situation seems ripe on the continent one reason being the fact that there is generally a generational gap between the leaders and young people. Demographically, Africa is a young continent with the majority of the population under the age of 30 while the leaders are on average above 65. The leaders in general have demonstrated an inability to listen to the youths and to incorporate their concerns and visions. Young people need leaders with whom they can communicate and speak the same language.

The Arab revolution has taught us that youths armed with courage of knowing that the status quo cannot continue can bring down pharaohs. The role of the youths today is no longer to demand more youth programs but to bring down governments that are no longer serving their citizenry (Ngugi, 2011: 9).

The role of the change agent is to challenge the people to a conviction that just as they are responsible for the creation of the present undesirable situation through their past decisions and actions or those of their parents, they are equally responsible for the creation of the future they want for themselves and for their children through the decisions and actions they make today. The grassroots must be convinced beyond any shadow of doubt that their predicament is self-made because they have the power to unshackle themselves. As in the words of Mahatma Gandhi, "Prisoner, tell me who was it that wrought this unbreakable chain? It was I, said the prisoner, who forged this chain very carefully" (Fischer, 1997: 163).

Robert Calderesi (2007) summarizes his book, *The Trouble with Africa*, by stating that African problems have been of its own making: dictatorial, kleptocratic governments, venal corruption, and poor economic policies and practices that strangled entrepreneurship, combined with cultural fatalism.

The Arab Revolution of the second decade of the 21st century is a clear example of this. The people, especially the youths crossed the threshold of pain and they were convinced that a good life was possible if the existing animal farm systems were destroyed. They understood that the people themselves are responsible for their own emancipation. No outsider could bring them liberation, and if they would wait for an outsider, they would wait forever.

A great obstacle to breaking animal farm systems is fear. It is upon fear that animal farm systems thrive. Fear is based on perceptions on who has the power. In the words of the Ugandan Scholar Mahmood Mamdami (Mbeki, 2000:149): "To understand the nature of the struggle and agency, one needs to understand the nature of power." In Africa, the citizens have remained amazingly passive in the face of bad rulers. Part of the explanation is their perception of who has the power. They see power as a zero-sum game in favor of the leaders and they have seen the leaders brutally wield that power. They see leaders employing neo-patrimonial "big man" chieftainship style of rule, dispensing favors and using all manner of tools to bolster their rule, from traditional governance structures to kinship ties and aspects including witchcraft and the Church (Mills, 2010: 213).

Conscientizing the people to reclaim and gain their power is the way to conquer fear.

When a people are inspired by a vision of a better future, and when that vision acts as a magnet pulling them as a people outraged by the pain of the present to the desired future, fear gives way to constructive action for change. Actual pain and anticipated pleasure are the driving forces behind change or the willingness to destroy animal farm systems. People will make sacrifices to any level if they are outraged by the current situation and anticipate the aspired future they aspire.

The message of the change agent therefore is simple: "This is what you can be, but this is what you are today. The power to be what you can be is in your hands; no one will take you there. If you make that decision and if you begin to move forward, no one will stop you."

Malcolm X challenged African Americans thus:

> Just because you are in this country (America) doesn't make you an American. No, you have got to go further than that before you can become an American. You have got to enjoy the fruits of Americanism. You haven't enjoyed those fruits. You have enjoyed the thorns. You have enjoyed the thistles (*Cambridge Editorial Partnership*, 2010:155).

Similarly people in Africa must be challenged on the meaning of citizenship and also on the fact that as long as they are not enjoying their rights as citizens, they are not full citizens of their countries.

For the change agent, it is important to engage ordinary people on what is keeping them from the life they aspire, the reasons, the issues and who is behind those issues. It is also the role of the change agent to guide the people to the support systems they may need if they decide to take action.

Young people need to be inspired by stories of possibility. They need to be told stories of countries like South Korea, Singapore and Malaysia which in relative terms have fewer resources than most African countries and at the time of independence were similar or worse off than most African economies yet today they are million miles away as far as progress and development are concerned. Young people also need to be told that they have bigger stakes in their countries because they will live in those countries longer than the older people. Young people need to be inspired to move beyond opinions to conviction on issues of social and economic justice. They need to move beyond mental agreement to courageously and fearlessly do something about it including offering their souls and bodies to the cause. Young people need to understand what citizenship means, what their rights as citizens are and compare this with their lived experience, and take deep discussions on how to bridge the gap.

In addition to raising consciousness among the young people, they must also be given concrete methods they can use to bring about the change they want. Non-violent direct action has been found to be more effective than most approaches. Among its methods are: mass demonstrations, willingness to go to jail in masses, prayer vigils, conscience fasting, boycotts and legal actions.

These are more effective when they are carried out simultaneously as a campaign.

Young people are a fertile target because they are worst hit by problems of underdevelopment. Societal change has mostly come through young people. The recent Arab Revolution is a classic example. The greatest developmental need for Africa today is the awakening of its young people. This is succinctly captured by Martin Luther King when commenting on the rising of young people against the segregation system in America when he said,

> A generation of young people has come out of decades of shadows to face naked state power; it has lost its fears, and experienced the majestic dignity of a direct struggle for its own liberation. These young people have connected up with their own history—the slave revolts, the incomplete revolution of the Civil War, the brotherhood of colonial black and brown men in Africa and Asia. They are an integral part of the history which is reshaping the world, replacing a dying order with a modern democracy (Carson, 1998: 135).

Different animal farm systems

Some animal farm systems are mild and they only need modification and alignment. The work required to do so is mostly lobbying for more democratic space and for more inclusion of different voices from the different stakeholders. Negotiation skills and compromise are key skills in this situation.

Some animal farm systems are extreme and are beyond redemption. The systems and the people that represent them have become hardened, recalcitrant, non responsive, arrogant and not willing to change. These are, in the words of Martin Luther King, "Old guards who would rather die than surrender." Extreme cases like Libya's Muammar Gadaffi in effect tell their people, "It's either I lead you or I kill you. Choose what you like."

What do people do when their governments become predatory and murderous? What do people do when governments, using their numerical strength in parliament, pass laws aimed at concentrating the power of the President turning him into a dictator in the process? What do people do when their Presidents believe they are God given gifts to their countries and therefore they can stay in power for as long as they want and when they decide to leave or die in office their spouse or some relative should succeed them? Negotiation and compromise does not work in this situation. Uprisings and revolutions become a developmental option.

When peaceful and non-violent means fail as was the case in Libya, armed struggle may be an option. After years of demonstrations, boycotts, strikes and civil disobedience against Verwoerd's apartheid regime, Nelson Mandela was convinced that the only alternative was to resort to violence. He came to believe that non-violence works with reasonable governments but may not work with recalcitrant animal farm systems like apartheid (Adebajo, 2010: 316). Similarly Franz Fanon, in his book, *The Wretched of the Earth*, made the observation that Africa had achieved "fake decolonization" leaving real power in the hands of foreigners and their "agents" among the ruling elites. He urged for an overthrow of the entire system using violence to achieve real, deep, fundamental and structural change as non-violence would not work in those situations (Meredith, 2006: 123, 147).

Resorting to violence is a very controversial point to comment on because in reality, there are hopefully very few situations that would justify the use of violence. At the same time, it is a common observation that violence breeds violence and the need for revenge. Fighting governments with organized armies is a formidable challenge for unarmed citizens. Appealing to people's minds and consciences through non-violent means remains the desirable option.

Political change happens at different levels: deep, deeper, deepest. Extreme cases as experienced in many African countries require extreme solutions. To date much of the human rights efforts are still struggling to demonstrate results at the deep level. The popular uprising social movements have consciously and consistently demonstrated results at the deepest level. What is going to take human rights NGOs and civil society organizations to make a genuine contribution towards change at the deepest level where it is needed most?

Sometimes systems can become too powerful and too pervasive than entire populations. This is usually the case in extreme autocratic regimes such as Zimbabwe. But even in autocratic regimes there is usually some room or space that can be taken advantage of with right timing. What is the difference between Tunisia and Zimbabwe, for example? What about Egypt and Libya?

All these were non-responsive animal farm systems that required a revolutionary hammer. What explains the success in Egypt and Tunisia as compared to Zimbabwe, and what are the lessons we can draw from that? A key lesson is that change is only possible when there is a balance of power. Autocratic regimes tend to concentrate too much power in the hands of the President. When the people assume more power than the state machinery, they can overrun it. If a government has too much power over the people, it will become recalcitrant and non listening. Absolute power corrupts absolutely. It is not possible to create a healthy society without balance of political power.

In *Animal Farm*, like all animal farm systems, they started with a healthy balance of power but as time progressed, more and more power was appropriated by Napoleon and his cronies. The anticlimax of *Animal Farm*, like most animal farm systems, is that the animals forgot that just as they reclaimed their power from Mr. Jones, they also could equally reclaim their power from Napoleon and his cronies, that just as they had removed Mr. Jones from the farm, they could also remove Napoleon from the farm. They had lost their capacity because of the gradual and continuous brainwashing and the growing myth of Napoleon.

Lessons for breaking animal farm systems in Sub-Saharan Africa

Levels of felt pain

In the Arab world there was an expression of felt pain and a demonstration that the pain had crossed the threshold. The revolution was sparked by an individual who set himself on fire in Tunisia, and another one in Egypt. Young people, women and even children braved bullets in resisting the animal farm systems. The people caught the spirit of revolution and freedom.

They were inspired by courage. They had reached high levels of conviction. They had conquered fear. They had settled the question of death. They came to the conclusion that sometimes it is better to die than live in oppression but if you die at least die fighting the oppression. They had conquered selfishness.
They had faith that if they died, their death would not be in vain. Their children would hopefully live in a better country that they had sacrificed for. They believed in the power of numbers. They believed that though unarmed the oppressors would not kill all of them, they would run out of bullets, and therefore victory would eventually be theirs. In the words of Marcus Garvey, they made the resolution that, "like men we'll face the murderous, cowardly pack, pressed to the wall, dying, but fighting back!" (Grant, 2009: 120–121)

Although it is appreciated that the Zimbabwean situation is not as spontaneous as that in the Arab situation, the levels of expressed pain cannot be compared. The pain that the people of Zimbabwe eventually suffered came as a result of the deteriorating situation due to the failings of Mr. Mugabe's regime or system, not the people's own deliberate pain expression for change. In other words, it was reactive pain rather than the proactive pain of the people in the Arab world.

An animal farm system cannot continue to exist if a critical mass of the people decides and acts to overthrow it. The reason the Arab spring was successful in throwing out Ben Ali, Mubarak and Gadaffi was that most of them had decided and acted to fight the system they represented. The reason leaders in Sub-Sahara Africa may not be removed even if they are no longer fit to rule is that the opinion of the people is divided—no critical mass has been reached. If 51% of the people decide and act, no animal farm system can stand.

Change happens when the collective pain of the people goes beyond loyalties to issues such as tribe, partisanship and religious affiliation. In other words, it does not happen when the pain is essentially human; change happens when the pain reaches a threshold. In the words of Dave Ramsey, "Not until the pain of the same is greater than the pain of change will you embrace change."

The people in the Arab world were focused and they knew what they wanted. They wanted the fall of the regime. They wanted the President and his whole system to go. Such levels of consciousness and focus are rare in Sub-Saharan Africa. Africans, Sub-Saharan Africans, are capable of so much pain and are easily satisfied with so little. This is why tyrants easily thrive here.

Social Cohesion

The Arab population was generally a cohesive society. They had few differences among themselves. The key issue at hand: the need for radical political change formed their common bond.

Zimbabweans, as are many in many Sub-Saharan countries, were divided. I remember talking to some middle class friends in Zimbabwe who insisted that yes, they would want Mugabe to go, but at the same time they would not want to be led by Morgan Tsvangirai because he was not "educated enough." The tie in the votes between Mugabe and Tsvangirai in the 2007 elections is part of the evidence of a divided nation.

I met a young man from Zimbabwe at the airport in Johannesburg, in South Africa. I asked him about his take on Mugabe. He told me he "appreciated" the gravity of the situation in Zimbabwe but personally he could not say anything against Mugabe. I asked why? He told me he was Ivorian. Some years earlier he had come to Zimbabwe to a conference. On the last day of the conference Mr. Mugabe came for the closing ceremony. Afterwards he found himself in a room where Mr. Mugabe was handing out scholarships to some Zimbabweans.

Mr. Mugabe asked him why he was not in the line with the others. He told the President that he was not Zimbabwean and that he was Ivorian. The President told him it does not matter as long as he was African. He gave him a scholarship to study for a PhD in America and promised to give him any job in Zimbabwe when he finished his studies. After finishing he came back to Zimbabwe and got a job of his choice given by the President. He went back to Ivory Coast to pick his family and became a Zimbabwean.

"For this reason, my friend," he told me, "I cannot say anything against Mr. Mugabe." I understood but wondered if favors done to us should blind us to reality and make us ignore justice. In much of Africa those close to power will scandalously defend it to a point that defies all reason.

South Africa, in many ways, is different. It is a country born out of protracted struggle against a very recalcitrant animal farm system called apartheid. The South African people are therefore very militant in defending their hard-won freedom. This observation withstanding, some commentators are also observing that though South Africa shines as a beacon, there are disturbing observations that the people-driven power can be hijacked. The consecutive governments of Nelson Mandela, Thabo Mbeki; and Jacob Zuma have created a black elite while the black majority population remains poor, still living in townships and are third class citizens in all but name. Although apartheid is gone, black oppression has replaced white oppression (Ngugi, 2011: 9). The system of oppression is still in place.

In many African countries these levels of consciousness are very low and issues of solidarity are not issues at all. Many countries on the continent have undergone transition without transformation.

Botswana has had the good luck of having generally good leaders who put the country before their self-interest. Being a small country it is relatively easier to plan services for the population and control the territory. Their leaders have managed to carve a niche in diamond and beef industries and invested the money in the development of the country. And more importantly, the country is held together by a national philosophy of the essence of being human—*botho*. The people therefore are generally united and peaceful.

Although the country has challenges with the relevant role of civil society in a situation where the government is generally performing, beside large infiltration of China and foreigners, it is one of the very few countries in Africa where people can stage serious and well staged demonstrations against government and government takes them and their demands seriously. Many

African countries do not have this capacity. In such countries, there are usually more observers than participants at campaigns or demonstrations. Such countries offer a fertile breeding ground for animal farm systems.

The role of religion

Siding with the poor and opposing their oppression by the powerful is a key role of religion in society. A religion that only talks about heaven and ignores daily realities is at best irrelevant and at worst dangerous. John the Baptist stood up against King Herod for abusing his power by taking away his young brother's wife. He paid with his life as a result. Dr. Myles Munroe argues that "since the number one need in the world today is good government as all problems in countries are caused by bad government systems, the number one politician in a country is the pastor because his or her job is to bring God's (just and righteous) systems into the country." The essence of the pastor's work and indeed of all spiritual people is to "bring heaven on earth" as said in the Lord's Prayer.

In the Arab Revolution, religion played a key role. Religious leaders played a key leadership role by marching in front of the people and through inspiring and encouraging sermons. In Egypt, Muslims and Christians and their leaders worked hand in hand in supporting the revolution. Fridays and Sundays became spiritual renewal days at the Freedom Square.

In Zimbabwe as in much of Africa, the role of the church was not as much as was in the Arab revolution. The church in much of Sub-Saharan Africa is perceived to be more of playing the "religious teaching and pacifying" role and not so much of empowering the people to deal with everyday issues especially those to do with bad governance.

In my experience, in much of Africa only the Catholic Church seems to have a conscious agenda for social/political change by action and beyond being only through "prayer and intercession." Real strategic spiritual warfare goes beyond just "prayer and intercession." During the years of looting and pillage of the Congo by Mobutu Sese Seko, the only organization that survived Mobutu and the looting was the Catholic Church. It was the only institution that could stand up to Mobutu (Dowden, 2009: 3690. Many churches seem to adopt a policy of "no confrontation with powers that be." They have adopted a policy of loyalty to the government of the day at any cost and as a result, the Church has largely lost its power and influence and has become a pawn for politicians.

The Christian church today is growing fastest in Sub-Saharan Africa and a "loyalty to the government of the day policy at any cost" stance is doing a lot of disservice to the church. Its greatest danger is in reducing the relevance of the church especially to the empowered and enlightened young people who expect the church to take a clear stand against animal farm systems in their countries. Eventually, this has a potential to stop church growth and the sustainability of the churches.

In *Animal Farm*, Moses, the raven, preaches of a sweet heaven though aware most of the animals on the farm were living lives far from satisfaction. This curse of hypocrisy is also the case in most religious leaders "bought" by animal farm systems in many African countries.

One day I was passing through Uhuru Freedom Park in Nairobi, Kenya, when I saw a group of people setting up a stage. I asked a colleague in the car what the meeting was to be about. He told me that the Kenyan politicians who had been summoned by the International Criminal Court to Hague to answer charges on their involvement in the post-election violence of 2007 were arriving that day from the Hague, and from the airport would come straight to the Park for mass rally prayers, to pray for them. It didn't make sense to me. I asked what the prayers would be about and what it was exactly the religious leaders wanted God to do in that context. My friend could not reply.

I have also always wondered if men and women of God of the past like the prophets in the Old Testament and not long ago, the likes of Charles Finney, Aiden William Tozer, Andrew Murray, Benson Idahosa and Kathryn Kulhman would ever accept "political appointment by Presidents or politicians" to serve the government. Being an advisor is another thing but becoming an "officer" with the aim of defending government policy, directly getting involved in the partisan political processes, is something else, especially when such an involvement is perceived by many to be controversial and divisive. The stand Rev Martin Luther King, Jr. took in relation to the government of his day, to oppose injustice, was not very different from that of the prophets of old. Men and women of God could do well to take a similar stand in Africa today. Men and women of God must always side with the poor and the oppressed; when they are too close to government, especially in Africa, it is not possible to speak for the people. Keeping quiet when the poor are being oppressed could be even worse than working directly with the animal farm governments as sins of omission are worse than sins of commission.

There is no question that religion has been used efficiently as a tool for empowerment, but it is also common knowledge that the same religion has been used as a tool for domesticating and brainwashing humanity. Listening to some phone in programs on the radio, I often get worried to hear how religion can promote fatalism and stifle activism in some people. I hear people say things like, "We should not rise up to protest because the government and its leadership are not to blame. What we are experiencing are just the 'signs of the times.' It was written in the Bible that these difficulties we are worried about will intensify in the last days. We are living in the last days, so it is normal to experience these problems. All we can do is pray." As a believer myself, I know this is misrepresentation of the Scriptures.

For one thing, the Bible says, "(In the last days) nation shall rise against nation, kingdom against kingdom; there shall be famines, and pestilences, and earthquakes in divers places" (Matthews 24: 7). These are mostly natural disasters beyond much of our control. And these problems are very different from the problems we are talking about. The Bible does not say there will be widespread poverty, constant electricity black outs, water taps that do not run, repression of human rights, forex shortages, leaders who want to stay in power forever, nepotism, mediocrity, etc. These are mostly by human construction, and have nothing to do with natural or divine design.

I believe the real mind of God is in the Lord's Prayer in which we are encouraged to pray: Our Father, Who art in Heaven, Hallowed be Thy Name. Thy Kingdom Come. Thy Will be done in the earth, as it is in Heaven . . . (Matthews 6: 8–9 King James Version). I am very sure that in heaven there is no poverty, electricity blackouts, water taps that do not run, repression of human rights, forex shortages, autocratic leaders, nepotism and mediocrity. This, according to the quoted scripture is the will of God for citizens of the earth including all Africans. God expects and uses human agency to replicate His heavenly kingdom on earth. Justifying suffering, doing nothing about it and encouraging fatalism is inconsistent with the nature of the Biblical God.

The Pentecostals and Charismatics are a growing spiritual and religious force on the continent but at the same time, they are the least "politically development conscious" group on the religious landscape. Pentecostals and Charismatics face the danger of being caught asleep and out of time with the true heart beat of modern African youths. If religion does not take its rightful political responsibility, the very freedom of religion they enjoy may be taken away and it may become difficult or impossible to praise the Lord freely as they do now. If we do not stand up against evil and make our stand clear we are colluding with the evil. It is rare in many African countries to find Pentecostal leaders who speak about rights from the pulpit and make it a priority to enlighten their people on the same. A good number of prominent Pentecostal pastors are too close to the powers that be, making it difficult for them to take a clear stand on crucial issues affecting the general citizenry. Some of them just don't want to rock the boat.

The character or true nature of a system becomes clear and distinguishable in times of pressure and crisis when taking a clear stand becomes imperative. In such times pretending becomes difficult. When a President declares that he is going to over-rule the constitution to stand for a third term in office when the constitution bars him from doing so, or when he imposes his brother or wife as his successor, the stand of systems and individuals in the country becomes clear. Silence in such cases is always deemed to be consent. In times of peace there is often a false sense of unity and people can pretend to be patriotic. In such moments even animal farm systems can pretend to be empowering systems. It is when the heat is on that the true character and nature of systems and individuals are manifested.

Martin Luther King, J., (Carson, 1998: 18, 19) summarizes the role of religion succinctly when he says,

> I feel that preaching is one of the most vital needs of our society, if it is used correctly. There is a great paradox in preaching: on the one hand it may be very helpful and on the other it may be very pernicious. It is my opinion that sincerity is not enough for the preaching ministry. The minister must be both sincere and intelligent . . . I also think that the minister should possess profundity of conviction. We have too many ministers in the pulpit who are great spellbinders and too few who possess spiritual power. It is my profound conviction that I, as an aspirant for the ministry should possess these powers.
>
> I think that preaching should grow out of the experiences of the people. Therefore, I, as a minister, must know the problems of the people that I am pasturing. Too often do educated ministers leave the people lost in the fog of

> theological abstraction, rather than presenting that theology in the light of the people's experiences. It is my conviction that the minister must somehow take profound theological and philosophical views and place them in a concrete framework. I must forever make the complex the simple.
>
> Above all, I see the preaching ministry as a dual process. On the one hand I must attempt to change the soul of the individual so that their societies may be changed. On the other I must attempt to change the societies so that the individual soul will have a change. Therefore, I must be concerned about unemployment, slums, and economic insecurity. I am a profound advocate of the social gospel.

In practical terms he is saying,

> (As a pastor), I took an active part in current social problems, I insisted that every church member becomes a registered voter and member of the NAACP and organized within the church a social and political action committee—designed to keep the congregation intelligently informed on the social, political and economic situations. The duties of the Social and Political Action Committee were, among others, to keep before the congregation the importance of NAACP and the necessity of being registered voters, and—during state and national elections—to sponsor forums and mass meetings to discuss the major issues (p. 47).

In the matter of fighting animal farm systems, many churches and their leadership need days of penance. They need to repent that they have failed God and their people through sins of commission and omission as far as their duty of keeping their congregations intelligently informed on political and governance matters are concerned. By emphasizing heavenly citizenship of the faithful, they have forgotten that as of now, the faithful are still earthly citizens and that they must exercise their citizenship to be good Christians or Muslims.

The gospel must be relevant to the social, political and economic life of man and it must respond to the context in which people are living. The gospel must guide people on how to deal with the political, social and economic realities and injustices of their daily lives. It must equip people to stand up against animal farm systems. If the gospel fails to do this, it becomes part of the problem rather than the solution to genuine human liberation. People with well developed critical faculties may find it difficult to associate with religious institutions that seem indifferent to injustices perpetuated by powers that be against the masses. They may also find it difficult to trust religious institutions that seem to be too friendly to powers that be which are obviously oppressing the masses.

Africans are very religious people. But their religiosity has not matched material progress. Observing a similar situation among the African Americans of the early 20th Century, Marcus Garvey observed, "We, the black people, have been very spiritual in the past; we are going to take part of the material now and will give others the opportunity to practice the spiritual side of life as well" (Grant, 2009: 186).

Steve Biko (1996: 64) summarizes this subject well when he states,

> To be relevant in Africa, Christianity must shift its emphasis of man's moral obligations from avoiding wronging false authorities by . . . not stealing food when he is angry and not cheating the police when he is caught, to being

> committed to eradicating all cause for suffering as represented in the death of children from starvation, outbreaks of epidemics in poor areas or the existence of thuggery and vandalism in townships. In other words Christianity must shift the emphasis from petty sins to major sins in a society, thereby ceasing to teach the people to suffer peacefully.

These are the issues that Christian pastors and preachers must begin to talk about seriously or risk Christianity from losing its relevance to the general public especially the youths. Steve Biko's (1996: 65) warning and advice to African pastors and preachers, "God is not in the habit of coming down from heaven to solve people's problems on earth," rings true today.

Willingness to sacrifice

A struggle without casualties is not deep enough. Any push towards change in the status quo will always attract a reaction. The attraction is always in the form of resistance. The resistance is often directed at persecuting the individuals championing the change. Persecution of the champions of change and sacrifice on their side are the logical expectations of any efforts aimed at bringing about change in the status quo. Only when the change being advanced does not threaten the powers that be will there be no repercussions and there will be no sacrifice.

A clear example is that to do with Muammar Gadaffi in Libya. What started as a popular uprising met with a brutal response from the oppressor who was in denial and was not willing to budge an inch. He declared a full fledged war against his own people. Many were killed but the people did not chicken out. They organized themselves to meet the naked government machinery unleashed on them. In the end, the masses won; Gadaffi was ousted and killed.

This level of response is rare in Sub-Saharan Africa but not impossible. In the fight for independence from the colonial masters, Africans showed the same type of zeal, determination and tenacity. But like in *Animal Farm*, many Africans have forgotten that just as they overthrew the colonialists, they can similarly oust the tyrants in the same way their colleagues in the Arab world have done.

A key challenge to overcome is personal comfort and thinking beyond "me, my spouse and my children." Among many African young people there is more complaining and false expectations that, as the American say, "George will do it"—usually referring to some NGO or civil society organization. There is also some naïve expectation that people like Mugabe and Gadaffi will eventually change and become good leaders. Nothing can be more naïve. These are oppressors and in them, the question of giving up leadership on a silver platter is just inconceivable. Confrontation is the only way to send their animal farm systems packing.

One indicator of development among people is their ability to say no to what is not in their interest, and their willingness to stand up and fight for their interests without giving fear room to usurp them of the determination. I believe that an important day to celebrate in a baby's or child's life is the one in which he or she has expressed a "no" for the first time; to me, this signifies a great developmental shift in life as far as asserting his or her own power is concerned.

Political consciousness

It is a human tragedy that we are often blinded to love our enemies and hate our friends without understanding the contexts in which this applies. For the people we think to be our friends, we usually let our guard off. If everyone were a friend in the sense we understand it, civilization would long have suffered terribly because terror would be left free in our world. Politicians are very good at utilizing this human weakness. It takes high levels of political and developmental consciousness to know who a friend is and who an enemy is; this principle also applied in politics.

The masses, especially the youths in the Arab Revolution demonstrated high levels of political consciousness. They demonstrated that they believed that the balance of power was in their favor. This was the major driving force behind their mobilization and action. This was also aided by technology—the internet, Facebook, twitter and cellphones. These acted as great catalysts for the revolution.

In much of Sub-Sahara Africa the levels of political consciousness or development is low. At demonstrations, there are usually more spectators than participants. Animal farm systems have managed to instill so much fear that people believe that the balance of power is against them and also that the animal farm systems in place are invincible and indispensable.

A colleague was talking to a group of students on self development. One student said, "We abandoned our plan to hold a demonstration because we were tipped off that if we went ahead the police would use live bullets against us." Such lies planted by animal farm systems entrench fear among the people. Animal farm systems use public media and informers for taming and domesticating whole populations through presenting the picture of governments as omnipresent and almighty. Unless such propaganda is dismantled through alternative sources of information, it will be very hard indeed for the masses to conquer their fear and rise up against animal farm systems.

Martin Luther King, Jr. once said, "Those of you who can read and think . . . must assume the leadership responsibility for educating our brothers and sisters." The responsibility rests squarely on the shoulders of enlightened and empowered young people, who in many countries in Africa, have unfortunately become disenchanted with politics because of lack of local political role models. Being described as dirty, politics in Africa is mostly left to people who are perceived to be "dirty" mostly corroborated by their bizarre decisions and actions as politicians. Bad governments take advantage of such situations to thrive and perpetuate themselves. Bad governments smile when the majority of the people in a country are illiterate, poor and incapable of critique.

When I was writing this book, I wrote a few friends in a number of African countries to ask them for information regarding the political situation in their countries. The common response I used to get was: "I don't know. I am not into politics." In fact, most of them were afraid because they said politics is a sensitive issue. These were professionals and university graduates but they were victims of animal farm systems. They had become part of the problem rather than the solution. Lack of political consciousness and development among the African middle class is a major factor maintaining animal farm systems on the continent. This group of people is potentially a great force in shaping the political destinies of their countries. By playing it safe, they leave this destiny in the hands of the many, easily manipulated, illiterate and semi-illiterate masses that need their guidance. Bad politicians are voted into power by good people who do not vote or who choose not to play their role in the political development and consciousness in their respective countries.

In 2007 I was part of the organizing committee of the group Concerned Citizens in Malawi. The aim of the social movement was to put pressure on opposition MPs in parliament who were using their numerical strength against government to hold the whole country at ransom until government agreed to meet their demand. They were going to block the passing of the national budget, they said. We mobilized a nationwide movement to protest and put pressure on the MPs and persisted until they relented.

Most of my close friends were surprised. “Politics is a dirty game,” they said, “why do you want to put yourself in trouble?” My response was that I am a development worker and that there can be no development without good politics. When a political situation so demands, we must put on hold all “development” and other professional activities and redirect our energies to correcting the political situation until the situation is resolved. Pursuit of development or indeed any work in a politically volatile environment is like mending chairs on the deck of a sinking ship, chasing mice in a burning house, your house.

It is not enough or sustainable to have an attractive spouse, beautiful children, state-of-the-art vehicle and house when everything around you is up in flames. *Problems are like fire, it always follows a standing bush.* Enjoying wealth when the rest of the people are in pain is a false sense of security. A great challenge in Sub-Saharan Africa is to inculcate and entrench political consciousness especially among young people and the attitude that in any situation the balance of power is in favor of the masses no matter how strong the power at hand is. It must be understood that it is the duty and responsibility of every person to recognize and fight any manifestation of animal farm systems at any level no matter the cost.

Today we have a real leadership crisis in Africa especially in the field of politics. There are too few role models. As a result young people with good intentions are not motivated to join politics. Those who do, imbibe the values of the present leaders already intoxicated. The result is the reinforcement and perpetuation of animal farm systems on the continent. I was talking to a friend from an African country on changes needed on the political landscape on the continent. “We need new and young leaders,” I said. She looked me full in the face and gave me a disarming laughter. “Know what?” she said, “We have a very young President in our country, a worse case by far; his predecessor, an old man, was an angel.” I kept quiet; she was telling the truth.

A key leadership issue is the ability to help the people at the grassroots level to grasp the issues at hand and to motivate them to do something about it. In Malawi, for example, no one clarified clearly to the masses what zero-deficit budget was all about. When the budget was announced by the President, focus shifted immediately from what led to such a budget to how to make the zero deficit budget work. In addition focus was narrowed to how to make the budget work rather than what options the people had in terms of their response to the budget. No one was able to put these issues in a language that the poor, hardest hit, would understand. The grassroots did not understand what the difference was between this budget and all other previous budgets. All they could see was the almost immediate skyrocketing of prices as soon as the budget was announced.

Poor grassroots people would understand better a metaphor like: There is a poor man who lives with his wife and children alongside a neighbor. The road to the place of work for the poor man passes through the lawn of the neighbor. The neighbor is concerned about the behavior of the poor man because he is constantly beating up his poor wife and children every time he comes back home drunk. The wife and children are living in fear. The neighbor raises these issues with the poor man. The poor man is so adamant and shows no remorse or any intentions to change his behavior. The neighbor, as a way of putting pressure on the poor man, blocks the road that passes through his lawn so the poor man should not pass through it on his way to or from work. Apparently, it seems the path through the neighbor's lawn is the only path to his place or work where he derives his livelihood. The neighbor, however, gives him an opportunity, assuring him he will open the passage once the poor man promises to cease all hostilities with his helpless wife.

The poor man is very proud and vows that he would rather stop going to his place of work and lose his source of livelihood than budge to the demands or request of the neighbor. In other words, he is saying he would rather starve to death than reform himself in terms of violent conduct. The poor man loses his source of livelihood. Left with no option, he turns to the family he abuses and asks the members to intensify raising income from the eggs their ten hens lay, to make for the lost income.

With a metaphor like this, we then can engage the grassroots in developmental dialogue, in a language they understand. Dialogue can be facilitated by such questions as: Was the neighbor wrong to express concern about the poor man's behavior? Was the response to stop going to his place of work from where he derived his livelihood just? What was the real solution to the problem: run a family on eggs from ten hens or mend relations with the neighbor? Should the family members accept his proposal to run the family on eggs from merely ten hens when there is a better means of livelihood from his formal work? What should the responsibility of the family members be in ensuring that there is a lasting solution especially on their financial welfare?

This is the type of language the grassroots understand and which can challenge them to action. In the Malawian situation, the people at the grassroots are suffered not because there was no money but because their government was incomprehensively stubborn. The people were paying for the sins of a few individuals who considered themselves old guards who would rather die than agree to terms of reconciliation. There is a general lack of leadership today in Africa to help the masses understand the issues so they should be able to articulate their demands so as to become part of the democratic process in creative and more conscious ways, beyond just voting. There is a great need to move beyond "human rights experts" talking on behalf of the people to real civic agency where the grassroots people organize to real social movements that can give enough and unrelenting pressure on animal farm systems.

Identifying and addressing real issues should be the preoccupation of every country. When a President rapes the constitution to extend his stay in power by abolishing term limits the discussion should never be how well or badly he is doing as President in his second, third or fourth term; heads should roll throughout on how to reverse the situation to the norm of two terms per President as provided for in the constitution. When a President imposes his wife, son or brother to succeed him, the discussion should never be how well or badly, the handpicked leader is performing but how to bring the country back to a situation where leaders are genuinely democratically elected.

In order to be effective, efforts aimed at destroying animal farm systems must be focused and concentrated. They must focus on issues that matter to the people on the ground. In addition, the issues must be strategic and symbolic in order to create leverage and a developmental shift. In other words, the issues must be important in nature so engaging with them will have a symbolic significance to the whole democracy and governance concept. Success in dealing with such issues will bring normalcy in that the success will have direct implication on the whole practice of democracy and governance in the situation. In addition, success would make a strong precedent for future action.

Leadership in fighting animal farm systems

It is the duty and responsibility of every individual to demonstrate leadership in fighting animal farm systems. I remember a meeting I recently had with some leadership guru I later asked a few engaging questions one of which on what should keep one who wants to change the world for the better awake at night. "Confronting the self and systems is what should keep such one awake at night," was her reply.

Development at the level of transforming societal structures and systems is a process. It may take long or otherwise but fundamental change is only possible when people change animal farm systems to more empowering ones. The problem with conventional development practice is that for a long time it has been understood to mean giving people such things as material wealth, information, knowledge and money. Usually, these do not go deep enough; and animal farm systems are very comfortable playing along these tactics as they do not touch the power structures. Because these tactics operate on the surface, animal farm systems continue to concentrate their power while dispensing material things to the people they oppress.

In order to cause real developmental shifts, it is important for individuals and groups to first confront the contradictions within themselves so that they can have a moral and developmental ground to confront the animal farm systems they are facing. It is also important to work with and support the positive elements, no matter how little, in the animal farm systems while at the same time confronting the negative elements. In extreme cases as in many African animal farm systems there will, logically, be more confronting than supporting work.

In many animal farm systems, conformity is encouraged and rewarded while independent thought and objectivity are punished. This is because objectivity and independent thought stand in the way of the leaders' evil agenda. In these situations, being a change agent is not for the faint-hearted; it is for those people with that will of iron. And because many cannot go this much, they tend to prefer the role of the bystanders. But the truth is, by taking a mere spectator stance in choosing not to confront the animal farm systems in your situation, you are, in essence, colluding with the systems, dangerous as they are. By doing nothing you are doing something—perpetrating their stay in power.

Confronting animal farm systems means confronting issues not the people therein. The problem is with the system, not the individual. The system is the mould. It will keep producing the same results no matter the person at the helm. So, unless the mould is changed the results will continue to be the same. When we name the issue we give it its own power and we avoid being personal. By naming the issue, we can also focus and concentrate our energy more wisely. We avoid haphazard fire fighting.

The ability to confront animal farm systems and support empowering systems is the true definition of leadership. Leadership is a choice; it is a choice to support developmental positive and helpful factors within oneself and the systems one is working for, and also to confront hindering factors within oneself and the systems one is working for. The biggest challenge in Africa is that we have leaders who have not consciously chosen to be leaders and are therefore not willing to confront the contradictions within themselves and in the systems they are dealing with.

Through supporting and confronting we expand the "developmental space" by shrinking animal farm systems and expanding empowering systems. What attitudes, values and behaviors within yourself need to be supported and encouraged? What attitudes, values and behaviors in the systems you are working with need to be supported? Which ones, within yourself, and in the systems need to be confronted? Are you going to take the decision to be a conscious leader?

Conclusion

Sub-Sahara Africa will never cross the developmental threshold to unleash her full potential unless we get sufficient numbers of people challenging the status quo. My personal conviction now is that the primary responsibility for development in Africa is not with the "leaders"—the politicians—but with the followers, the ordinary citizens. I put the burden of this responsibility squarely on the shoulders of the empowered and enlightened young people. By this I mean those who are in or have attended secondary, high school and university education. If mobilized and organized, this group of people can create a critical mass capable of causing a significant and irreversible developmental shift away from animal farm systems to more empowering systems on the continent.

As of now we, as countries or the continent as a whole, have not agreed on who will take leadership in the development agenda. Of course, there are some who strongly believe that governments or to put it more bluntly, politicians, will bring development to Africa or African countries. I do not subscribe to this for one simple reason: though not all African politicians could be selfish or ill motivated, the majority of them are. Put simply, as most of them are running animal farm systems, they tend to become part of the developmental problem rather than of the solution.

Animal farm systems must be identified, surfaced, confronted and removed, to replace them with more empowering ones. In an era where through technology the truth cannot be hidden, animal farm systems need to spend more and more and sometimes impossible energy just to survive. With the flood in awareness and consciousness, these systems are heading towards extinction. The sooner the masses realize this truth, the better able they will exorcise the demons of this process.

The hope for Africa lies in the ability to identify, surface and confront contradictions in the animal farm systems present in African countries. Inability to do this will make oblivion triumph over utopia on the continent. If Africa fails to move beyond changing individuals rather than the systems the individuals create or represent, Africa will continue to move in cycles of developmental illusion and frustration.

Mass mobilization efforts that remove a Ben Ali, a Hosni Mubarak or a Muammar Gadaffi may not change the system completely but at least they can create a power shift between the leaders and the followers in favor of the followers. They can create a precedent.

I will conclude with the words of Martin Luther King, Jr.:

> These are revolutionary times; all over the globe men are revolting against old systems of exploitation and oppression. The shirtless and barefoot people of the world are rising up as never before. The people that walked in darkness have seen a great light . . . We must move past indecision to action . . . If we do not act, we shall surely be dragged down the long, dark, and shameful corridors of time reserved for those who possess power without compassion, might without morality, and strength without sight (April 4, 1967).

For democracy and good governance to prevail in Africa, animal farm systems must die and there must be eternal vigilance from the new generations to watch against their resurrection.

CHAPTER 8: CONCLUSION: TWO APPROACHES TO ORGANIZING AGAINST ANIMAL FARM SYSTEMS

Introduction

This chapter will conclude the book by discussing mass mobilization and "positive advocacy" as two complementary approaches for confronting animal farm systems. Poor people need liberation at the spiritual, mental and physical levels. Mental liberation comes mostly from mass education. Once a certain level of mass education has been reached, it is time to move to the next stage: physical liberation through campaigns. Campaigns are usually short term efforts though gains from them need to be sustained. An alternative and complementary approach is "positive advocacy." This is a long term approach aimed at building the people's economy with the aim of giving them "something worthy defending and fighting for."

Campaigns

The aim of the campaigns is not merely to mobilize people to action; the aim is to change both people and the systems. If change does not happen, it means the campaign has failed. When the wind of the campaign blows over a land, the face of the land must change.

The greatest challenges for the 21st century include how to tap and vastly expand the civic talents and energies of whole societies so as to address the many problems now, problems no expert system or government can begin to fix by themselves; and how to reverse patterns of civic decay and regenerate the civic muscle. In short, the greatest challenges lies in how to support initiatives that change cultures of poverty and despair into places of agency, abundance and hope (Boyte, 2010: 96). The movement against slavery, colonialism and racism shed some light. They looked hopeless at the beginning, but built slowly and surely, gaining momentum over time. They took a long time to bear fruit, but perseverance was the key. They succeeded through a mix of political action, real politics; and mass education, mobilization and action (Sachs, 2005: 364).

Drawing from the American civil rights movement of the 1960s, there are eight main elements which are key for successful campaigns against animal farm systems. Below is a full discussion of these elements:

1. Seize the moment

Evil systems are usually too strong to destroy from outside; however, they usually have an internal self-destruction mechanism. By becoming increasingly insensitive to the needs of the people they claim to serve, such regimes carelessly make decisions and take actions that have the effect of squeezing the people against a wall until there is no more space for them to breathe let alone escape. At this point, humanity reaches the threshold of pain and endurance, and it naturally reacts. This is the point that can be used as an emotional spark to initiate direct action against the system. It is difficult to get people involved if they do not have an emotional attachment to the issue or when they are not experiencing maximum pain and are not able to associate maximum pleasure with the envisaged solution after their involvement.

The spark knocks the people at the grassroots level from their slumber, instilling in them the urge to action, real action. The spark is more effective if it is presented as a death-and-life issue or an appeal to their human dignity and sense of legacy. This releases the collective energy for action. It is the basis for inspiring the people to become militant enough for direct action and at the same time sober enough to avoid disruptive eruption.

The Arab Revolution was triggered by the self-immolation act of a young man by the name of Mohammed Bouazizi as an expression of extreme frustration with the regime. The act had resonated with the general mood of the country and the whole region. The rage that ensued became the trigger that eventually changed the face of the Middle East.

2. Clarity on what the issue is

It is important to get all the facts right. It is important to articulate the issue in a way that the grassroots can get moved into action. It is important to focus on one key issue at a time. This ensures maximum concentration of effort. In the case of the Arab Revolution, the issue was the worsening living and economic conditions among the poor.

The issue must be of central importance so that people can rally around it. Issues of rising costs of living which are directly linked to bad governance must form the central thrust of the struggle. This is the most visible form of injustice of animal farm systems—leaders living in that opulence that defies reason when the masses hang on to life and survival in some kind of hell-on-earth state. Focusing on single issues increases the power of concentration. The issues addressed must be around the fundamental issues of justice, recognition, self determination and solidarity among the grassroots people. Firing people up to mobilize around an issue and take action is hard work because of entrenched fatalistic attitudes among the masses. Extreme views like the one expressed by an Ivorian editor below are not uncommon:

> This continent is really cursed. We may even have to accept that Africans are a bad copy of the human race. We always make ourselves look ridiculous in the eyes of others . . . what have we done, for our creator to pour such uncompleted beings to this planet? We can only wait for evolution to change us. Until then, all we can do is cry (Calderesi, 2007: 62).

Many Africans would rather die in poverty than rise up to fight for a better quality of life. A real need on the continent today is capacity for the rural and urban masses to stand up against corrupted and unjust governments. There is a great need to translate the slogan: *power to the people* into reality in order to make the campaign truly the people's.

Through acting and mobilizing on key concrete issues, citizens learn and acquire new identities as political actors; they become conscious of their rights and their rights to have rights. It is action that creates the sense and practice of citizenship as citizenship is created from below and it is not given from above (Gaventa, 2010: 65). From this observation we can conclude that many African countries do not have citizens in the real sense of the word, and for this, their leaders are always grateful.

Where people are very poor the only rights that matter to them are those economic in nature. Gandhi put it rightly when he observed that some people are so poor that God can only appear to them in the form of bread. To these people the only meaning of development is economic freedom. Campaigns are likely to be more successful when they attack the economic power structure rather than the political power structure. Politics must be backed with economics. There are so many educated young people but there are no jobs. There is a great untapped potential of the young people. There is great need to re-channel the energy of the young people so that we can expand growth and ensure broad-based economies.

This said, it is important to emphasize that governments have a duty to ensure political freedoms, economic facilities, social opportunities; transparency guarantees; and protective security (Matlosa, 2010: 128). Prioritizing the economic issues should be seen as deliberately symbolic, strategic and leverage implications on the other rights; and kind of sending a strong message of precedent to the authorities on what the masses can and will do against injustice in the other areas as well.

The success of a campaign hinges on the credibility of the issues being raised and the facts backing them. Driving home the fact that there is no freedom for the masses if there is no economic freedom is a key for awakening and inspiring the masses. Letting them know that they are under economic occupation mostly due to poor governance by their leaders is a great catalyzing in galvanizing the people to action. Onyeani (2000:51) emphasizes the point well when he says,

> The whole African race is under economic occupation. You cannot achieve true political independence without at the same time achieving economic independence. The so-called political independence we think we have now is merely an illusion. It is without solid foundation. A house without solid foundation is bound to crumble sooner or later. Without economic independence, sooner or later we will be recolonized politically. (Maybe we already are.)

3. Organization

Key to successful campaigns is organization. Organizing and mobilizing the masses to action against dominant powers becomes the facilitation of the emergence of consciousness. It gives the masses power which becomes the capacity to make decisions with maximum awareness (Kaplan, 1996: 65).

There is usually a need for a minimal structure to give order and direct the campaign. The organization must be built on a clear vision of what the people want to achieve. Key elements of the structure would be: an executive committee led by a charismatic leader who becomes the symbol of the movement. This must be a person of strong conviction and high level integrity as he or she is the personification of the values of the movement. The person also needs to be a good, strong and inspiring communicator able to rouse the people to action and at the same time keep them sober enough to avoid violent eruption. Leaders must be people of high integrity with no tainted past and of unquestionable motives. They must be leaders who are connected with the people's values, and they must have legitimacy. Their relationship with the people must be transformational and not transactional.

According to Peter Senge (1990: 359) leaders of campaigns and movements need highly developed leadership disciplines which include:

- Systems thinking—Thinking in terms of systems, complexity, interconnectedness and holism rather than in a simplistic or linear ways.
- Personal mastery—Ability to consciously move beyond opinions to concrete convictions. A leader without conviction cannot inspire.
- Conscious and progressive mental models—A personal vision of an ideal society in contrast to the reality on the ground.
- Building a shared vision—Soliciting people's aspirations and ability to communicate the emerging shared collective aspiration of the people with conviction and inspiration.
- Team learning—Ability to connect with the "mood" of the people and constantly aligning them to the vision. It also means becoming the personification of the values of the campaign or movement and encouraging the others to do the same.

The grassroots in Africa have tales of frustration and disillusionment from similar past efforts where campaign leaders got sold out to the very animal farm systems they had set out to fight. People need to be assured that they can trust the leadership. In the words of Holland,

> God give us leaders!
> A time like this demands strong minds, great hearts,
> True faith and ready hands;
> Leaders whom the lust of office does not kill;
> Leaders who possess opinions and a will;
> Leaders who have honor; leaders who will not lie;
> Leaders who can stand before a demagogue
> and damn his treacherous flatteries without winking!
> Tall leaders, sun crowned, who live above the fog in public duty and private thinking (*Washington*, 1991:143).

It is important to get support and direct involvement of distinguished people in society. In Egypt, individuals like Wael Ghonim, a popular and influential internet blogger became an inspiration to the masses and greatly energized the people when he joined the protests.

What gave Martin Luther King more authority and marked him as great was that he never asked, never encouraged, never even suggested that someone else engage in a battle that he himself was not prepared to lead personally (Jones, 2008: 45).

The executive committee can also double as the strategy committee. This committee is custodian of the vision of the movement and is responsible for identifying key issues needing attention and advising on how to address the issues. Key areas of concern include organizational capacity, activities to implement; and building alliances and relationships. Other committees include:

- Programs committee—This committee is responsible for planning and organizing campaign activities with guidance from the strategy committee. The programs committee is also responsible for managing communications. In the modern era, the internet, Facebook, twitter and cellphones are playing an increasingly important role in facilitating campaigns against animal farm systems. They can be used to mobilize people and coordinate whole cities or countries. This is an effective way of circumventing governments' tendency to monopolize national media—radios, TV and newspapers, and also the tendency to threaten withdrawal of licensees from independent media houses perceived not towing the government line. It is also important to note that though technology is a great catalyst, it cannot and as much as possible should not replace physical and face-to-face meetings. It is the morale built through actual gatherings which creates unstoppable momentum for the campaign. The programs committee also takes responsibility for teaching the masses the concept of citizenship—their rights and obligations especially as far as the issue at hand is concerned. They are also responsible for teaching the people the approach or philosophy upon which the campaign is based.
- Fundraising committee—For campaigns to be successful, they need a lot of money. The responsibility of the fundraising committee is to finance the campaign primarily from the contributions of the grassroots themselves. This increases the people's commitment to the cause. The committee also makes general and targeted appeals to the concerned citizens within the country. It is also the responsibility of the committee to get money from sources outside the country. The campaign will need money to, among other things, finance the program activities, meet transport costs and legal charges for those who get arrested. They will also need money for media coverage.
- Transport committee—Mass direct action has great transport requirements. The transport committee supports the programs committee in facilitating movement of the people. They assess transport needs and find ways of meeting the needs for the activities organized by the program committee.
- Legal committee—in the course of the campaign there will be a lot of legal battles and hence the need to have team of legal experts and lawyers on stand-by.

It is very important to understand the people's past and present attitudes towards militant non-violent direct action. Some communities need to be knocked out of their slumber of fatalism, hopelessness and helplessness while others will simply need a spark. People need a convincing and inspiring story that they can understand and relate to in the simplest terms possible. This must be based on a bright, vivid, concise and inspiring vision of what the change they are fighting for will bring. Africans are mostly preoccupied with the here and now. Most African countries do not seem to have a sense of a national vision or an aspiration of their country's place in the world. They are too preoccupied with the day's survival or bread and butter issues. Invoking a sense of vision is a powerful tool for mobilizing the people.

Another crucial point is the role of music in the campaigns or movements. Music plays a very powerful role in generating interest, inspiration and building momentum for the campaigns. Solidarity songs are particularly relevant. Popular songs that appeal to the young are also very important. Every movement has been propelled and energized by high morale music. Music also helps to attract attention to the cause of the movement. In addition to the role that music plays during actual campaigns, protest music plays a key role in maintaining a culture of health critique against powers that be. Songs like, Bob Marley's "Rise Up and Stand Up for Your Rights" do a good work in playing such a role.

By organizing the people in this way, we are promoting civic-driven change. The task of civic-driven change is advancing principles of genuine democracy—citizen control over public authority. The challenge is to advance civic agency primarily from the grassroots (Fowler, 2008). This is the way to restore the relationship between governments and citizens from the current *I—It* to the *I—Though* relationship—a relationship based on recognition and respect of the humanity of each other (Buber, 1958).

Leadership fails in Africa today because citizens do not individually and collectively engage consciously with the state to claim their rights. Civic-Driven Change needs to be given ascendancy in Africa as we are increasingly witnessing the failure of representative democracy. We witness parliamentarians abusing their position by passing bills that are meant to punish and disempower the people they claim to represent. Civic-Driven Change puts the development responsibility on the shoulders of every citizen. Civic-Driven Change provides the practical application for the concept of popular participation which has been defined as "the mass involvement of the people in the social processes of society including the political and economic realm. It is how people participate . . . to influence decisions that affect their life chances" (Adejumobi, 2009: 66).

Developing a culture of Civic-Driven Change is the way of destroying animal farm systems and replacing them with genuinely empowering and democratic systems. Politically involved citizenry are the backbone of long term sustainable development (Moyo, 2009: 58).

4. Agree on options for change and action

Different situations will require different approaches but recalcitrant animal farm systems will usually understand the language of militant direct action. The success of direct action depends on having large numbers of the grassroots. In Egypt, it was what they dubbed "The day of rage," 28 January, 2008, when a massive number of people turned out at the Freedom Square. That turned the tide of the campaign in favor of the protesters.

If the masses are not there it is difficult to proceed. *One person is gossip, many are a voice.* The louder the voice, the more unstoppable it becomes. The real victory in fighting animal farm systems is in the people at the grassroots level coming out en mass in a new sense of dignity and destiny. This is what will overwhelm and astound animal farm systems. This is what shifts the balance of power in favor of the people. This is what makes animal farm systems wake up to the fact that *ants united can lift up a dead elephant* and that *cobwebs united can tie up a lion.*

In addition, campaigns must seek to involve all age groups. A key constituency is university students, high school and secondary school students. Helping these groups understand their civic responsibilities practically is a significant contribution to a democratic culture in society. Franz Fanon however pinned his hope of mass effort to overhaul animal farm systems on rural grassroots masses. He regarded workers in towns as a "labor aristocracy," too compromised by the colonial or animal farm system to be of real use (Meredith, 2006: 147).

Militant non-violence is a universally acknowledged approach that has been used successfully in many places especially in India and America. The main merits of militant non-violence include disarming the opponent as he is meeting a foe without any physical weapons, exposing the enemy's moral inadequacies, weakening the enemy's morale, working on his conscience and providing a method for struggle to secure moral ends using moral means. Armed struggle is never commended unless the government decides to initiate a civil war as was the case in Libya. The protesters had to take arms in self defense and to protect their own people who were being systematically killed by the government. Many animal farm systems will crack and crash in the face of militant and direct non-violent action. The Arab Revolution, especially in Tunisia and Egypt, has demonstrated that authoritarian governments can be brought down through peaceful determined mass uprisings (Ngugi, 2011: 9).

Means to employ in militant direct non-violent action include mass rallies, peaceful demonstrations, boycotts, stay-at-home strikes on a mass scale, mass non-cooperation, prayer vigils, sit ins and jail ins. These work better when they are used in combination.

In taking militant direct non-violent action do not be naïve; be very sure that animal farm systems will strike back. There is usually a cost for taking leadership in fighting animal farm systems. Martin Luther King, Jr., (Phillips, 1998: 261) identified five predictable methods that animal farm systems will employ to disrupt campaigns aimed against them:

- They try to negotiate the leaders into compromise. Sometimes they offer money or opportunities to bribe the leaders. If that does not work,
- They try to divide the leadership. They employ the old fashioned divide-and-rule technique. They spread false rumors about the leaders to create doubt among the followers. They also try to establish petty jealousies and suspicion among the leaders themselves. If this does not work,
- They move to a get-tough policy through trumped up charges for the leaders, arrests and threats. If this does not work,

- They turn to actual physical violence—actual attacks on the leaders, "organized" accidents and "predictable fires and bombings" at their houses by "unknown individuals." If this does not work, they finally,
- Resort to mass indictment through mass arrests, actual shootings to kill as was the case in Libya, Bahrain, Syria and Yemen; and mass rape for women.

Threatened animal farm systems can take their reaction or opposition to extreme ends. Before taking on animal farm systems each leader must face the question of death and deal with it. In very extreme cases, each extra day that a leader fighting animal farm systems lives is actually a bonus.

5. Dialogue/negotiation

The purpose of the campaign activities is to create tension and bring pressure on animal farm systems so that space can be created for dialogue. Animal farm systems will only open up for dialogue when they feel the heat, when they are convinced that their own survival is threatened. This is why campaign activities must be of such a magnitude that the animal farm systems are left with no option but to call for dialogue and negotiation.

Campaigners must have clear demands as a basis for dialogue. During the Montgomery Bus Boycott in the 1950s in the US, the protesters gave three clear demands as a basis for dialogue and negotiation. The African Americans would not resume riding the buses until:

- Courteous treatment by the bus operators was guaranteed;
- Passengers were seated on first come, first served basis—African Americans seating from the back of the bus towards the front and whites seating from the front towards the back; and
- African American bus drivers to be employed on predominantly African American routes.

The demands must be clear, reasonable and significant enough to cause developmental shifts on the issue at hand. They must also appeal to the conscience of the good people in the animal farm systems. Every system no matter how evil has some goodness in it that can be appealed to. The demands must aim at changing power structures between the grassroots and governments. They must aim at creating structural changes that shift power in favor of the grassroots.

A key demand by the people at the grassroots level that will become significantly important will be constitutional reviews as many constitutions on the continent have been so tampered with that they no longer contain the spirit that represents the will of the people. In some countries, constitutions serve only one person: the ruling President and his party. When campaigns to oust animal farm regimes through direct mass action or through the ballot are successful, the first task for the new regime must be to bring the constitutions back to their original form. This is the first indicator that the new regime is not another animal farm system.

6. Monitor results

Sometimes animal farm systems will agree to the demands of the protesters just to get relief and space to regroup and restrategize. Their adherence to the agreements in this case will be temporary. It is important to make it clear that the militant direction non-violent action will be called in again should it be perceived that some of the agreements are not being adhered to. In extreme cases, for instance, where the citizens are calling for the fall of the regime, mass citizen action will never stop until the regime gives way to a new regime and leadership.

7. Empathize with those in power

Relationships are a key to the success of any endeavor. To ensure effective mobilization of citizens to successful action, it is important to stand in the shoes of those in power to understand their motivation or lack of it to give the masses the space they need and what they are demanding.

Some of the key reasons for lack of political compromise may include fear of loss of power, being unconvinced about "what is in it for them," power, civil society-state relations, and entrenched corruption or patronage among the power holders. Other factors constraining effective mobilization and action may include lack of capacity of government actors, lack of appropriate mechanisms illustrated by a general lack of practical checks and balances and also an entrenched undemocratic culture; and lack of citizen capacity to organize effectively. Another set of factors may include political leaders and bureaucrats feeling no sense of obligation or duty to listen, to respond or to account to ordinary citizens (Malena, 2009: 273).

Depending on the specific context and nature of the situation at hand, a number of strategies can be employed to strengthen political will. Among these are strengthening familiarity and trust between the state actors and leaders of the citizen movement, seeking and agreeing on a middle ground, as much as possible opting for critical collaboration rather than direct confrontation; not only flagging problems but also new ideas and solutions. In addition, political will can be enhanced by backing up arguments and proposals with reliable evidence; demonstrating mutual benefits to the power holders and the citizens of the outcome sought; and most importantly, empowering and mobilizing the citizens to ensure sustained pressure on the power holders (Malena, 2009: 278).

8. Sustaining victory

The most dangerous time is always immediately after success. In the heat of the excitement victory can be hijacked as has happened in many countries. At the beginning of the campaign it is important to have the blue print of the "new order" desired in place. The content of the "blue print" should concentrate on a clear description of all the changes we want to see from the "old older." This is the way of breaking the pattern of the animal farm systems and replacing it with a more empowering one.

Lobby and advocate for activities aimed at entrenching a democratic culture. Widespread poverty among the masses is major hindrance to cultivating a democratic culture. Poverty makes poor people compromise democratic principles at the altar of personal survival, forcing them to vote for corrupted but rich candidates. It is not only the poor masses who are manipulated, the legislators too are under pressure to pass bills that are in the interest of the regime or risk facing reprisals. Too often the bills are not in the interest of the common citizen. There can be no sustained empowerment of citizens if they continue to be shackled by poverty. Economic empowerment activities must form part of long-term democratic development processes.

It is difficult to organize and mobilize the poor masses when literacy levels are very low. It is also difficult to mobilize and organize those who went to school when citizenship education efforts are low or non-existent. In this situation people find it difficult to understand the issues at hand and they become easy prey for manipulators.

Many countries on the continent are in serious need of constitutional reviews to seal all the loopholes inserted by animal farm systems. Make sure the constitution is truly a people's living document. There is also a need to emphasize that major constitutional changes should apply only to the next government not the same parliament proposing the changes to discourage self-serving tendencies.

The ultimate aim of civic action is to make "people power," the "fourth arm" of government with the aim of balancing power relations in favor of the poor.

Positive advocacy

I first met Professor Jesse Mugambi on Thursday 26 April, 2012 at Jacaranda Hotel in Westlands, Nairobi, Kenya. We met at six p.m. By the time we were parting it was already 11 p.m. I guess we parted because we were reminded that the hotel lounge where we were sitting had to close. We had even forgotten to order our dinner. It had been a very long time since I had such an experience—a first and very intense meeting lasting five hours non-stop. An instant bonding with somebody I was meeting for the first time.

I got connected to Professor Mugambi by a mutual friend of ours, Mr. Harold Miller, a retired American missionary living in Nairobi. Harold introduced Professor Mugambi to me as a Theologian and a publisher. But as I was to discover that evening, in my opinion, he was much more than my earlier conception of theology. As an "indigenous wisdom-based organization development practitioner" by the end of our meeting I got a new understanding and appreciation of the relevance and importance of "applied theology" to the situation and context of Africa.

Whence and whither Africa?

The central issues of our discussion that night centered on a number of questions: Where Africa is today in her journey of development; what lessons we have learnt where we are coming from; what our destination is and what it shall take to arrive there. These are big questions which have generated a diverse of opinions over time.

As a theologian, Professor Mugambi's method is to use biblical metaphors. "In the story of Exodus (the journey of the Hebrew people from captivity in Egypt to the promised land in Canaan, a land flowing with milk and honey)—where is Africa today—50 years after independence?" he queried, repeating what he had once asked a group of fellow theologians at one time. "Are we still in Egypt under Pharaoh's oppression, or is Moses having a show down with the Pharaoh, forcing him to 'let my people go' or are we before the Red Sea, or walking on dry land inside the Red Sea or on the other side of the Red Sea? Are we just about to enter the Promised Land—the land flowing with milk and honey?"

The story of Africa is a complex one and the question—Where are we?—has no easy answers, and usually alludes any attempt at arriving at a consensus. What seems to be a point of agreement is that Africa is on a journey, but not on where Africa is coming from or is going. Other mind-boggling questions are: Who is determining the future of Africa today and in whose interest is he or she shaping that future? Who is determining the political, economic, technological and socio-cultural future of Africa today? Just to give an illustration, it is much more expensive to fly to Mozambique from Malawi (a neighboring country) than it is to fly from Malawi (a country near the southern tip of Africa) to the UK. This means it is easier for valuable resources including humans to flow from Africa to Western countries than within the continent. Many times, people from different parts in the same country or neighboring countries in Africa have to use a Western language to communicate. Africa is the only continent in the world where official business has to be conducted in English, French or Portuguese. Africa has been bleeding valuable resources to the West for over 500 years and it is naïve to think that the West would be happy to see Africa become more "self-defining" and less dependent.

The failure of NGO advocacy work

In the era of public governance and partnerships, non-governmental organizations have come to present themselves a force to reckon with in many issues as regards service delivery to the people. But the question is: non-governmental organizations, especially international NGOs a force for good or otherwise on the continent?

Non-governmental organizations have added value in service delivery to poor communities; they have made somewhat impressive contributions in the areas of water supply, health, agriculture, HIV and AIDS, disaster relief, etc. However, NGOs, especially international NGOs have not fared well as far as advocacy is concerned. Some people including NGO leaders are candid enough to confess that advocacy, especially the "structural change" type of advocacy is not and is not supposed to be the work of international NGOs. But recognizing that all the work done at the grass roots level, in terms of service delivery will amount to nothing if "power structures" are left intact, NGOs and donors may prefer to fund local NGOs to do the "agitating" work. The challenge in this arrangement, however, is that *when you borrow somebody's legs, you will always go where they direct you.*

International NGOs and donors often dictate what the advocacy issues must be. A striking example is the way the gay issue is being handled. David Cameroon declared that British aid will be tied to African countries accepting gay marriages which as of today are being considered to be against most cultures in Africa. This "foreign imposed" structural change advocacy has generally failed in Africa. Gay people as a minority have always existed in Africa and there were effective traditional mechanisms of dealing with the issue. Instead of identifying and recognizing these traditional mechanisms, NGOs and donors are imposing a purely Western approach to the issue. This is an example of the failure of good intentions of Western donors which may, unfortunately, create the impression that Western donations to NGOs is nothing but attempts by Western governments to destabilize Africa.

Social change is only possible if it is based on existing cultural foundations. If you introduce change based on other cultures, it may survive but for a short time. *The river that forgets its source will soon dry up.* Social change is not a science or technology (though it uses these); it is anthropology. If you get the anthropology wrong, everything goes wrong. This is why many a time projects begin to falter once an expatriate leaves.

A key evidence of the failure of International NGO-led development is lack of sustainability of their projects. In other words, the flow of benefits from the project often ceases when the project closes. On a more political level, many NGOs have floundered when management changes hands from expatriate to locals. The only development that is sustainable is endogenous development. No person can develop another; all development is self development. In other words, a person can only develop himself or herself. Similarly, a community can only develop itself; the same applies to an organization or even a country.

Positive advocacy—a model for genuine development work in Africa

There are endless examples of people coming together around common needs and fight for their rights in communities all over the continent. The real essence of the work of civil society is to organize around alternative values that contribute to shaping living systems that are more sustainable (Taylor, 2012). This is the story of Utooni Development Organization in which Professor Mugambi is a board member.

We visited UDO on Saturday, 28th April, 2012. About three hours away from Nairobi, UDO is in Machako's district. In observing and analyzing the UDO story, I came up with seven main points that set it apart from most conventional international development initiatives. These points are what constitute Professor Mugambi's concept of "positive advocacy"—a model which he believes points to what development work on the continent must look like. He defines positive advocacy as "alternative ways of doing things which are positive—showing it can be done using what we have." It also means saying no to what we do not want in a positive way, and more importantly, empowering the people to have something to live for, defend, and if necessary die for.

The following are key characteristics of positive advocacy in the Utooni case:

1. The organization is based on locally felt priorities and initiatives by the poor masses. Machakos, the district in which the initiative is located, is a dry area. The rivers run dry as soon as the little rainfall stops, if it falls at all that year. Lack of water is therefore an agreed need and priority by all the people in the area. Only those initiatives that meet the real needs of the people will be supported. *The best mouth to tell you a hat has bed bugs is that of a person who lives in that hut.* It is the people themselves who can tell what their real needs are. The initiative was organized around sand dams meant to preserve and make water available throughout the year.
2. Local leadership—development initiatives rise or fall on the type and quality of leadership. Leadership simply means the application of vision. The founder and pioneer of the organization had a vision that can be summarized in the biblical phrase: the desert shall rejoice. His famous quotation was the biblical verse: "Where there is no vision, the people perish." This was a real vision backed by passion, conviction and action and not just a mere dream. The vision was shared among all members of the community with an evangelistic zeal. There was a strong realization that to bring about change, it is important to attempt to involve all including the slowest in community. The organization was "community interests and not money-driven." The people came together to solve a real problem not to "attract donor funding." Joshua Mutikusya, the founder, was true leader of his people. He led by example. He took the most risks including persecution and imprisonment. He bravely fought detractors and would-be hijackers. Most importantly, he embodied and personified the values of the people he led. He stood for something; he stood for the interests of the people. This gave him unparalled legitimacy and connection with the people.
3. The organization was rooted in the people's culture and values. It was based on the local concept of *mwethya*—a localized version of *ubuntu* which simply means we can only succeed by working together because *in hostile times you cannot survive alone.* We need others and each other. Everyone in the community must make a contribution by their ability, age, gender, etc. The principle is that everyone in the community has a contribution to make except the very old and the very young. Values of honesty, accountability and transparency are held in very high esteem. Those who violate these values are punished in a way that will teach the others a lesson. A number of people who violated these values had their names taken off or erased from a wall where the names of all organizational members are written. This is not meant to shame them but traditionally it makes a very strong statement of disapproval of their behavior. Song and dance are part of the work.

The question, Who are we and what do we believe in? is a fundamental tenet of genuine development work and change. One of the principles of the sand dams is "to use only the water that you need and let the rest flow on to others downstream." This is in great contrast to the insatiable capitalistic greed which is one of the major contributions to global poverty.

4. The organization's initiatives are long-term rather than short-term in nature. The initiative began in 1978 and is still on-going. The people in the communities have integrated the initiatives into their own lives. The initiatives have become part of their culture. They do not have "deadlines to meet" and for a long time they did not have "reports to write," "to be accountable to some donor." Ownership and legitimacy have been enhanced because people know that the initiative will always be there for them. It is not a project that will come to an end some day soon.
5. Joshua Mutikusya knew that development work does not do politics but is politics—albeit a different type of politics from conventionally construed. When a donor made an offer to give them some maize in a year of drought, Joshua and his team demanded that they should know the source of the maize. He was insinuating that they did not want to be given genetically modified maize. He tasted imprisonment for the role he was playing in bringing about "consciousnesses among his people." He also knew how to "handle" powers that be. When approached by an international seed company, he asked for a "fair partnership." They never came back. He believed that for development to happen the parties involved must engage each other as "a strong person to a strong person" and not "a strong person to a weak person." He also knew that one ought to be very wise on how they say no to the powerful. He knew that it is dangerous to tell the king that he is naked but there must be a way, a wiser way of communicating the same.
6. A key sustaining factor for the organization's initiative was the tangible and concrete benefits. Through the sand dams, the people are able to grow crops throughout the year, a thing that could not happen before. A group I visited is now constructing a building for income generation. While they used to access water for a few months in a year, now they can access water throughout the year through the sand dams. Agricultural output in the district has significantly increased. They used to "import" almost every food commodity. Today they are a net "exporter" with many people coming from elsewhere to buy from them.
7. The most impressive aspect of the Utooni initiative is the scale of its achievements. As soon as I entered the catchment area, I was overwhelmed by the vastness of their initiatives—a rare feat I have never seen in almost all evaluation assignments I have undertaken. The sheer vastness of the scale is almost a miracle—maybe one of the wonders of Kenya. To date the initiative has constructed 1,500 sand dams at an equivalent cost of Kshs 1,738, 928, 304 with a total value of water in each sand dam estimated at Kshs 10,000,000. The average number of beneficiaries per sand dam is 1,000. The total terrace dug by the initiative in meters is estimated at 1.5 million.

A recent evaluation show that the initiative has:

- Decreased distance to get water (one way) from an average of 10 km to only 1 km
- Decreased time to get water from an average of 12 hours to only 1 (hour)
- Significantly increased the number of farmers planting trees, digging terraces, planting indigenous drought resistant crops, practicing no till and zero grazing; and
- Significantly increased the variety and yield of food being produced

One day, walking around the area, 25 years after he had started the initiative, Joshua complained about young men burning bricks.

"Can't you see that this means an economy is emerging in the area? Twenty five years ago, we could not talk of burning bricks in this area because there was no water. The bricks are an indicator of our success," Professor Mugambi pointed to him.

In addition, the number of men idling and spending all their time drinking has gone down. This capacity to change people's values and negative behaviors is rare among development initiatives.

"What drives these people?" I asked Professor Mugambi. "The future," he told me. He clarified this further by stating that without spirituality and *ubuntu* or *mwethya* one cannot do development.

"The spirit of *mwethya*," he said, "is what is driving this initiative—you can see the people singing and dancing as they work. You can see the people working without pay."

Honestly speaking, no economics, science or technology could do that.

Challenges for the future

The Utooni story demonstrated that it is possible to achieve success without following foreign imposed steps. And that transformation is possible—bare hills, for example, are being covered again with trees. Most importantly, these people cannot be manipulated or be bought by politicians.

The first phase of Utooni Development Organization ended with the passing away of the pioneer leader, Joshua Mutikusya in late 2011. Most of Joshua's friends—the ones he worked with since 1978—have moved on. A few are still in the board. The management of the organization has mostly been handed over to a new generation of young development workers with academic qualifications. A key question is, "How long will the original vision and values which were rooted in endogenous and self reliant development, survive and excel?"

As the organization faces the immediate future, three key issues and dilemmas come to mind: the danger of being captured by NGO-ism and its values, how to ensure continuity of the original vision and values; and the danger of undermining community values with increased urbanization.

Poverty is an orphan but success has many relatives. The phenomenal success of UDO has and will continue to attract many interested partners who would like to be associated with the success. Non-governmental organization donors are happy to be associated with successful NGOs such as UDO. A key challenge arising out of this is that many times donors come with their own conditionalities which may undermine the organization's agenda. Joshua showed great courage and wisdom in minimizing donor dependency and ensuring "adult to adult" relationships in all discussions and engagements with donors. In the post-Joshua era there is a perceptible increase in reliance on donor funds. How this may affect the identity, agenda and the values of the organization is the question. Besides, how well will the organization continue to be community rather than donor centered?

Of great importance is the question of preserving the original vision of the organization. *There are so many good things in life but they are not all meant for you.* Joshua Mutikusya knew the few good things meant for him and UDO at that time. Concentration and maintaining focus on what really matters to the people they serve will be a real test of the capability of the new leadership and the custodian role of the board. There is usually a temptation to get "easy donor money" from donors which may not serve the need to meet our real priorities.

Preserving the spirit of *mwethya* in a changing social context will also prove to be a great challenge. Traditional values of community and cohesiveness usually hold in rural settings. With increasing urbanization, partly resulting from UDO's own success, the leaders will have to find ways of preserving the *mwethya* values. A group I visited started with 120 members. Now there are only 32. Among the young staff, what will persuade them to entrench the conviction that this is not just a job, but a calling or a vocation and that one can't go wrong by doing right?

Beside increased urbanization, there is the question of the inevitable change of priorities of the people from purely social needs to economic needs. UDO will remain relevant if it responds well to this transition. The next step might be value addition and processing to increase and diversify the farmers' income. But how well does the current staff profile respond to this new need? What extra skills and competences do they need and how well can they afford or support such needed changes?

The biggest problem in Africa is poverty. Anything that does not address the immediate needs of the people is irrelevant as far as the people are concerned. Animal farm systems thrive in situations where the majority of the people are too poor to care. Once the people go through the political and economic empowerment process as is happening in Utooni, political oppression and manipulation is no longer possible because ignorance, powerlessness and fear have no effect on them.

With sufficient strategic thinking and foresight the above challenges and dilemmas are not insurmountable. As it is today, UDO stands out as a model of an endogenous development initiative that can point to how development work must be done it Africa.

The answer to where Africa is in her journey of development lies in what the Africans themselves are doing about it.

Conclusion

No one can understand the African situation better than the Africans themselves. Others can only see us from the outside; as a result they may not go deep enough in surfacing the issues we face and how to address them. *It is the people who live in the house who know that there are bedbugs in the house.* A truly African-rooted and African-driven developmental agenda can only be created by the Africans themselves. It is important to emphasize that this will not be achieved by the people who have made "development" their career—the people who are part of the "development industry" that is now in many cases part of the problem rather than the solution. The torch bearers of the *anti-animal farms movement* will be genuinely concerned citizens, in large enough numbers to cross the needed threshold or tipping point. Most of the times these people will be guided by "enlightened" youths who have said, "Enough is enough," and mean just that. The isolated beacons of success like Botswana, Mauritius, Malaysia, Singapore and South Korea bear witness to this. Imported formulae have mostly disappointed us. To be successful this movement will need to be based on post-colonial knowledge and post colonial practice emerging from these beacons of success. Africa will never develop building on the wisdom of Europe and America and the agents of their system acting as leaders in Africa. Africa will only develop building on the foundation of her own endogenous wisdom.

If there is one lesson we should learn in Africa, it is that passage of time without human agency cannot and does not change animal farm systems into anything better. Many times, time itself without human agency becomes an ally of animal farm systems. Vigilant and conscious human agency, not from a few expert groups, but from the masses, is what destroys animal farm systems. With an average age of 25 years on the continent, young people will have no one to blame but themselves if they do nothing about opposing, fighting and defeating animal farm systems.

Not long ago, the former Tanzanian President, Mr. Benjamin Mkapa, warned: "The way things are, we, in Africa, will soon have no image beyond geography, no identity beyond color and no decency except flags" (Eyinla, 2007: 85). The warning stands true today. Africa's hope is expanded civic space occupied by the grassroots. Measures for poverty or development need to shift from basic needs such as access to food, shelter and clothing to citizenship indicators such as the ability to know one's rights, privileges and obligations as a citizen and putting this knowledge to work in one's interests as an individual and as groups.

"Development," stripped to its bare essentials means the ability to say no. It is the ability to say no to what is not in public interest. It is the ability to say no, not only with words but also with action when necessary. Development is the ability to say no to broken promises, no to nepotism, no to tribalism, no to fear, no to mediocrity, no to concentration of too much power in the hands of leaders, no to elected leaders not respecting their terms or tenure of office, no to manipulation; and no to abuse of power in all its forms.

BIBLIOGRAPHY

Achebe, C. 1983. *The Trouble with Nigeria*. Heinemann: London.

Adebajo, A. 2010. *The Curse of Berlin: Africa After the Cold War*, University of Kwazulu Natal Press: Scottsville.

Adejumobi, S. 2009. The African Experience of Popular Participation in Development. In Adejumobi, A and A Olukoshi (eds). *The African Union and New Strategies for Development in Africa*. Dakar: CODESRIA Books.

Biko, S. 1996. *I Write What I Like*. Rivan Press: Johannesburg.

Boyte, H. 2010. Civic Driven Change and Developmental Democracy. In Fowler, A & Malunga, C. (eds). *NGO Management: The Earthscan Companion*, Earthscan: London.

Buber, M. 1958. *I and Thou*. T & T Clark, Edinburgh.

Calderisi, R. 2007. *The Trouble with Africa: Why Foreign Aid Isn't Working*, Yale University Press: London.

Cambridge Editorial Partnership, 2010. *Speeches that Changed the World*. Quercus Publishing Plc: London.

Cammack, D. 2009. The Politics of Chameleons Revisited: The Burden of Malawi's Political Culture. In Kanyongolo, F and Ott, M (eds) *Democracy in Progress: Malawi's 2009 Parliamentary and Presidential Elections*, Kachere Series: Zomba.

Carson, C. 1998. *The Autobiography of Martin Luther King Jr*. Warner Books, New York.

Chachage, C. & Cassam (eds), C. 2010. *Africa's Liberation*, Fountain Press: Kampala, Uganda.

Diamond, J. *Collapse: How Societies Choose to Fail or Survive*, Allen Lane, Penguin Group: London.

Dowden, R. 2009. *Africa: Altered Sates, Ordinary Miracle*. Portobello Books: London.

Easterly, W. 2007. *The White Man's Burden*. Penguin Books: New York.

Eyinla, B. 2007. Democratization and Governance in Africa. In Mohamoud, A (ed) *Shaping a New Africa*, Kit Publishers: Amsterdam.

Fischer, L. 1997. *The Life of Mahatma Gandhi*, Harper Collins Publishers: London.

Fowler, A. 2008. Beyond Civil Society: Civic Driven Change, Paper Presented at the INTRAC International Conference, 3–5 December, 2008, Soesterburg, the Netherlands.

Gaventa, J. 2010. Seeing Like a Citizen: Reclaiming Citizenship in a Neo Liberal World. In Fowler, A & Malunga, C. (eds). *NGO Management: The Earthscan Companion*, Earthscan: London.

Gilles, J and Alvarado, F. 2012. Country Systems Strengthening: Beyond Human and Organizational Capacity Development—Background Paper for the USAID Experience Summit, USAID: Washington D.C.

Grant, C. 2009. *Negro with a Hat: The Rise and Fall of Marcus Garvey*, Vintage Books: London.

Guest, R. 2005. *The Shackled Continent: Africa's Past, Present and Future*, Pan Books: London.

Harden, B. 1990. *Africa: Dispatches from a Fragile Continent*, Harper Collins Publishers: London.

James, R and Malunga, C. 2006. Organizational Challenges Facing Civil Society Networks in Malawi, *Knowledge for Development Journal* Vol. 2 no 2 pp 15–18.

Jones, C. 2008. *What Would Martin Say?* Harper Collins: New York.

Kapiriri, M. 2011. Unleashing Africa's Unique Human Resource Potential: Dismantling the Historical Mould, Paper Presented at the 2011 International Human Resources Management Summit, Nairobi, Kenya.

Kaplan, A. 1996. *The Development Practitioner's Handbook.* Pluto Press: London.

Lamb, D. 1987. *The Africans.* New York: Vintage Books.

Langer, A, 2010. Ivory Coast's Elusive Quest for Peace: IBIS Discussion Paper No. 4 in *Discussion Series: Patterns of Conflict Resolution.* Available online www.ucd.ie/ibis/publications/discussionpapers/cotedivoireselisivequestforpeace/#d.en.75028.

Malena, C. 2009. *From Political Won't to Political Will: Building Support for Participatory Governance*, Kumarian Press: Sterling, USA.

Mandela, N. 2010. *Conversations with Myself.* Macmillan: London.

Mapanje, J. 2002. *Gathering Seaweed: African Prison Writing.* Heinemann: Oxford.

Mbah, F. 2011. Militants Dilemma, in *BBC Focus on Africa*, April–June 2011.

Matlosa, K. 2010. The APRM and the Promotion of Socio-Economic Development in Africa: Whither Popular Participation? In *Peering the Peers: Civil Society and the African Peer Review Mechanism*, EISA: Johannesburg.

Maxwell, J. 2008. *Leadership Gold.* Thomas Nelson: Nashville.

Mbeki, T. 2000. *Mahube: The Dawning of the Dawn.* Skotaville: Braamfontein.

Meredith, M. 2006. *The State of Africa: A History of Fifty Years of Independence*, Jonathan Ball Publishers: Johannesburg.

Mills, G. 2010. *Why Africa is Poor and What African can do about it*, Penguin Books: Johannesburg.

Moyo, D. 2009. *Dead Aid: Why Aid is not Working and How there is a Better Way for Africa*, Farrar, Straus and Giroux: New York.

Munroe, M. 2009. *Overcoming Crisis: The Secrets to Thriving in Challenging Times*, Destiny Image Publishing: Shippensburg, PA.

Nasser, G. 1955. *Egypt's Liberation: The Philosophy of the Revolution*, Public Affairs Press: Washington D.C.

Ngugi, M. 2011. Cairo to Cape Town, in *BBC Focus on Africa Magazine*, April–June 2011.

Ogwang, T. 2011. Root Causes of the Conflict in Ivory Coast, *Backgrounder* no.5, April 2011.

Hochschild, A, 2011. Explaining Congo's Endless Civil War, *The New York Times*, 3 April, 2011.

Onyeani, C. 2000. *Capitalist Nigger: The Road to Success*, Jonathan Ball Publishers: Johannesburg.

Phillips,D. 1998. *Martin Luther King,Jr. on Leadership: Inspiration and Wisdom for Challenging Times.*Warner Books. New York.

Randeira, S. 1996. The Crisis of Developmentalism: Some Remarks on Culture, Political Processes and Population Policies, in *Development Models and World Views*, German Foundation for International Development: Frankfurt.

Rodney, W. 1971. *How Europe Underdeveloped Africa*, East African Educational Publishers: Nairobi.

Sachs, J. 2005. *The End of Poverty: How We Can Make it Happen in Our Lifetime*, Penguin Books: London.

Shapiro, R. 2008. *Future Forecast: A Global Vision of Tomorrow.* Profile Books. London.

Senge, P. 1990. *The Fifth Discipline: The Art and Practice of a Learning Organization*, Currency Double Day: New York.

Senge, P., Scharmer, C., Jaworski, J., & Flowers, B. 2004. *Presence: Human Purpose and the Field of the Future*, Society of Organizational Learning: Cambridge.

Taylor, J. 2012. *Struggles against systems that impoverish: South African civil society at the Crossroads*, CDRA: Cape Town.

Thomson, S. 2011. On Genocide Anniversary, Rwanda Needs Political Reform, *Africa Portal.*

Washington, J (ed). 1991. *A Testament of Hope: The Essential Writings of and Speeches of Martin Luther King Jr.* Harper Collins: San Francisco.

Yew, L. 2000. *From Third World to First.* Harper Collins: New York.

INDEX

Chiku Malunga is the first and leading Indigenous Wisdom Based Organization Development (IWBOD) writer. He holds a doctorate degree in Development Studies from the University of South Africa. He is currently the director of CADECO (Capacity Development Consultants), an organization that promotes African-centered organizational improvement models.

Malunga's other books include: *Understanding Organizational Sustainability through African Proverbs*; *Making Strategic Plans Work: Insights from African Indigenous Wisdom; Understanding Organizational Leadership through Ubuntu; Oblivion or Utopia: The Prospects for Africa, Power and Influence: Self-Development Lessons from African Proverbs and Folktales, Cultivating Personal and Organizational Effectiveness: Spiritual Insights from African Proverbs;* and *NGO Management* (co-edited with Alan Fowler).

www.ingramcontent.com/pod-product-compliance
Ingram Content Group UK Ltd.
Pitfield, Milton Keynes, MK11 3LW, UK
UKHW020147290926
15471UKWH00004B/734

9 780761 864363